Multinationals in Western Europe:
The industrial relations experience

Multinationals in Western Europe: The industrial relations experience

International Labour Office   Geneva

ISBN 92-2-101476-2

First published 1976

HD
69
.I7
m8

Printed by Imprimeries Populaires, Geneva, Switzerland

NOV 15 1976

TABLE OF CONTENTS

PREFACE

The following report was based largely on field survey interviews conducted in some six West European countries, Belgium, France, the Federal Republic of Germany, the Netherlands, Sweden and the United Kingdom. It is recognised that there are significant variations in the industrial relations systems of all countries; but since time and resources dictated, in part, what could be done, these six countries were chosen in the belief they could present a useful comparative, cross-section view of the subject under study.

In addition to limiting the study largely to these six countries, there has been a concentration upon the food (and related) industries and the metal industries. For metals, interest was focused principally upon the engineering industry, and particularly its automobile and electrical-electronics sector. On occasion the study ranged beyond these industries but the original conception was that the food and metal industries would offer a wide and varying range of comparative experience, so far as multinational company labour relations were concerned.

In all countries meetings were held with the central employers' and union organisations. Additional interviews were conducted with officials of the metal manufacturing (engineering) employers' associations and the metalworking unions. Similar meetings were held with officials of food employers' associations and food manufacturing unions. Interviews were also conducted in different countries with officials of some leading food and metal manufacturing multinational companies as well as with local union officers or works council officials representing workers at particular multinational companies. In most countries contact was also made with government officials with responsibility bearing upon the subject under analysis.

The ILO expresses its great appreciation for the generous time and assistance rendered by the many persons who were contacted in the course of the study. It acknowledges the collaboration of Mr. Everett Kassalow who carried out the study.

To facilitate matters a list of questions and issues was prepared and sent in advance to those to be interviewed. These "questions" were largely open-ended, and designed to guide the discussions, rather than serve as a quantitative oriented questionnaire-survey. The "questionnaires" varied slightly from country to country, and were also modified during the course of the inquiry as new issues suggested themselves. Separate lists of questions were submitted to union and management interviewees, but for the most part the ground covered was similar. At the time the meetings were held in Sweden, these lists of questions were still in a preliminary state, and interviews in that country were conducted without advance circulation of the lists. Subsequently, some additional conversations and correspondence were carried on with a few Swedish union and management representatives. (Sample copies of the questionnaires used in several countries are included as Appendix I to this report.)

While the study is based primarily on the field surveys, use has also been made of the literature on this same subject, and appropriate citations can be found in many parts of the study.

Readers should keep in mind that this study has been limited to the union-management or industrial relations aspects of multinational subsidiary plants in Western Europe with particular emphasis on collective bargaining. The attitudes held about these companies may stem from other parts of their activities, such as those which relate to problems of taxation, expatriation of profits, political activities. Of necessity, this study has sought to isolate the industrial relations aspects of multinational enterprises, but in real life this distinction may be rather artificial.

It should also be pointed out that limited as it has been to developed countries in Western Europe, the labour experience of multinational enterprises here described may not necessarily be characteristic of similar companies' experience in less developed countries. At a later date it is expected that a companion study of such experience in selected less developed countries can be completed.[1]

----

[1] The largest share of direct company foreign investment appears to be in Western Europe. According to the United Nations, some 68.2 per cent of direct foreign investment, at the end of 1967, was in developed countries. If one takes

(Footnote continued on next page)

The first seven chapters of this report deal with specific major areas of the industrial relations experience of foreign-based multinational companies (union recognition, the role of multinational managers in employers' associations in the various countries surveyed, etc.). The final chapter presents an overview of the study, in the form of its major findings and conclusions.

(Footnote continued from previous page)

the distribution of overseas affiliates of multinational corporations by area, the same report indicates that for selected developed market oriented countries, their multinational companies affiliates abroad were distributed as follows: 73.6 per cent in developed market economies and 26.4 per cent in developing countries. See United Nations, Department of Economic and Social Affairs, Multinational Corporations in World Development: ST/ECA/190 (New York, 1973), tables 11-12, pp. 147-148 (estimates are for the end of 1967). For the United States, by far the source of the largest volume of direct investment abroad (close to 60 per cent of the total of developed market countries), in 1970 direct investment in Western Europe was $24.8 billion. This compared to $22.8 billion in Canada and $16.1 billion in other areas. US Department of Commerce, The Multinational Corporation, Studies in US Foreign Investment, Vol. I (Washington, D.C.: US Government Printing Office, 1972), tables 1 and 3 (pp. 9 and 13). The important links between many major US and Canadian unions make the transnational labour relations of those two countries a special case. As regards manufacturing companies, the prime focus of our study, the concentration of direct foreign investment in Western Europe is even greater.

CHAPTER I

MULTINATIONALS, UNION RECOGNITION
AND RELATED PROBLEMS

A useful starting point in a survey of industrial relations in multinational subsidiary metal and food plants of Western Europe is the status and extent of union recognition in such plants. This ILO survey reveals that in a very large majority of cases unions were recognised by the management of these plants; but the same survey also reveals important exceptions to such recognition, in two countries, as well as instances where recognition was achieved only after much more difficulty than is normally experienced with national firms.

Union recognition difficulties in multi-nationals in the United Kingdom

Difficult union recognition cases with multinational enterprises have been more numerous in the United Kingdom than in other countries surveyed, but there are also several significant "cases" of recognition difficulty in the Netherlands as well. One important multinational enterprise also posed a recognition problem for unions in Sweden in the past.

As far as the United Kingdom is concerned, the work of John Gennard[1] generally supports the conclusions which flow from the field work done in connection with this ILO report. A number of multinational engineering, chemical and food companies have withheld union recognition in the United Kingdom. It is added, that they "adopted paternalistic stances toward their employees and attempted to check demands for unionism by the payment of relatively higher wages and the provision of good fringe benefits".[2]

Some British firms of course also resist recognising unions; but certainly among firms of the general size of multinationals they are relatively fewer. The British Trades Union Congress (TUC) has charged that "a substantial number of foreign-owned firms have refused trade union recognition ... they tended to take a much more systematic anti-trade union line than British firms in the equivalent position."[3]

One must take into account that there is a tendency for trade unionists and others to react with great sensitivity to multinational enterprises as compared to national companies, in some situations.[4] Even a handful of difficult cases[5] may make
----

[1] See his studies, as follows: "The Impact of Foreign-Owned Subsidiaries on Host Country Labour Relations: The Case of the United Kingdom", in Robert J. Flanagan and Arnold R. Weber, editors, Bargaining without Boundaries: the Multinational Corporation and International Labor Relations (Chicago, University of Chicago Press, 1974); Multinational Corporations and British Labour: A Review of Attitudes and Responses, British North American Committee (London, Alfred H. Cooper and Sons Ltd., 1972), and also with M.D. Steuer, "The Industrial Relations of Foreign-Owned Subsidiaries in the United Kingdom", British Journal of Industrial Relations, Vol. IX, No. 2, July 1971, and a chapter with Steuer in John Dunning, Editor, The Multinational Enterprises (London, 1971, George Allen and Unwin, Ltd.).

[2] Gennard and Steuer, BJIR ..., op. cit., p. 154.

[3] Trades Union Congress, Report on a Conference on International Companies, Congress House, London, 21 October 1970, p. 8.

[4] Gennard and Steuer, BJIR ..., op. cit., p. 155, note "When trouble over non-recognition arises, with a foreign-owned company it tends to get greater union and press publicity and has perhaps created the impression that domestic firms are less anti-union than the foreign company. Whether this is true or not, it is the case that the foreign company often starts big in this country, altering the recognition and the power relations between the employer and the unions, compared to domestic firms."

[5] The TUC cited especially Kodak, Roberts-Arundel and Caterpillar Tractor, Trades Union Congress, Report on a Conference ...., op. cit., p. 9.

them appear as though all or nearly all multinationals have been difficult on the matter of union recognition. The fact remains, however, that if one examines manufacturing in the United Kingdom, it is possible to list a number of large foreign-owned subsidiaries which have not granted union recognition or did so only after a long struggle. Among British employers of anything like comparable size, during the same period (reference is made especially to the post Second World War era), one can find only a few similar cases.

As Gennard and Steuer observe, the multinationals arrive in a foreign country with great resources, and are better able to resist unions than can most British employers which often "have grown up here from small and weak beginnings ...".[1] Moreover, the multinational may enjoy greater flexibility, including, in some cases, the possibility of using sources of supply outside the country of immediate implantation. At the least this may seem a threat to the workers in the foreign subsidiary.

In the Netherlands the number of large firms that withhold union recognition is quite small. A few multinational subsidiaries, however, stand out conspicuously in engineering and in petroleum. Dutch unions deeply resent this state of non-recognition in a country where union recognition has come to be widely accepted, especially for larger plants.

It also appears to be significant that the most conspicuous engineering firm in this regard in the Netherlands is one which still withholds union recognition in the United Kingdom. The same company at first also resisted union recognition in Sweden, where such tactics seemed bizarre to unions and the employers' associations.

This company, it might be added, also does not recognise any union in its home US-operations, and is almost unique among comparable engineering firms in the United States in having no unions at any of its plants. It can be added that US-based companies which resist unions in Western Europe are usually among those who have not recognised, or barely recognise them in the United States.[2] One hastens to note, however, that there are a few companies which have a "poor" record as regards union recognition in the United States, but have accepted union recognition abroad without great difficulty.

US multinationals and union recognition problems

It has been for the most part some US multinationals which have difficulties with the issue of union recognition. This stems, where it occurs, in part from the somewhat "special" nature of the union recognition process in the United States itself. John Shearer writes, "Some American corporations have inappropriately transferred their home-grown convictions about union recognition and union security to overseas environments ...". Thus, at home US firms often refuse "to recognise [unions] until the Wagner Act" with its exclusive election process compels "them to do so". Shearer observes that "Where there is no legal obligation to recognise unions, as in the United Kingdom ..." some US firms have "precipitated major problems" by failing to understand that "in some industries custom dictates automatic recognition through association agreements ...".[3]

Several multinational food enterprises operating in the United Kingdom indicated that future recognition of unions, especially for white-collar employees, on their part, would be contingent on the unions' demonstrating a 51 per cent following. Most of these enterprises had at one time been members of their relevant employer associations, but this was no longer true.

The British Trades Union Congress has stated, on the sometimes difficult matter of US firms' attitudes on union recognition, that this in part reflects the situation in the United States, "where only 22 per cent of the labour force is unionised, as against 42 per cent in the United Kingdom". In addition:
----

[1] BJIR ... op. cit., p. 158.

[2] One can also cite the case of one French-based chemical-rubber firm which unions find difficult in that country. This same company is conspicuous among rubber tyre manufacturers in North America in having resisted union recognition.

[3] John Shearer, "Industrial Relations of American Corporations Abroad", in S. Barkin et al, International Labor (New York, Harper Bros., 1967).

... United States firms operate at home under the National Labor Relations Board regulations and are accustomed to delaying recognition until they are legally obliged to by elections conducted by the NLRB. This contrasts with the "voluntarism" of British industrial relations ...[1]

This same point about US companies and their previous experience with the National Labor Relations Board was made about several engineering firms which have withheld union recognition thus far, and in one US-based food firm. A similar explanation was suggested for the withholding of union recognition by another food manufacturer until recent years when an effective organising campaign was directed against its plants.

In another case, a US multinational opened a plant in Scotland, but refused union recognition. A thirteen-week strike ensued, and it was only after the union struck at another plant of the same company, that "recognition was eventually granted".[2]

US companies sometimes seek some concrete indication, such as a majority vote, to the effect that their employees want a union to represent them, and some also have their own conception that such a relationship should be constructed with no more than one union representing any single group of employees (a plant, an occupation, etc.). The imprint of US union recognition procedures in some multinational plants in the United Kingdom has therefore been felt in a different way. Several US firms have recognised unions but have sought to avoid the problems of multi-unionism so characteristic of much of British bargaining, especially in engineering. They have done so by signing what have been called "closed shop agreements with particular unions and insisted that these are the only unions employees can join ...".[3]

Multinationals in development areas

Union recognition issues can be particularly troublesome in so-called development or less industrialised areas or regions, where government is seeking to accelerate economic growth. Here where unionism is less well established, where a "new" working class is recruited, unions may have greater difficulty in organising plants of multinationals who come with some of their own conceptions about union recognition. The work of Forsyth on the recent industrial relations experience of Scotland seems to suggest this.[4]

Dutch unionists note that even their relatively few, but to them significant, difficult problems of union recognition with multinational firms tend to centre in and around the general Rotterdam area. Here in the post-1950 period, a large number of foreign multinationals poured in, and they were not always easily assimilated in what proved to be a great industrial expansion area. This was unlike the case, it is argued, of Amsterdam where older working-class and industrial relations structures stood up more to new companies. A number of US and British-based petroleum and chemical companies tended to make their own industrial relations way in this Rotterdam area, and in several cases did not even recognise unions.

Even where union recognition is not at issue, the entrance of a multinational into a special development area can become a troublesome labour matter. Some of the difficulties which Ford Motor Company encountered with Belgian unions in the Genk

[1] Trades Union Congress, Report on a Conference ..., 1970, op. cit., p. 8.

[2] Ibid., p. 9.

[3] John Gennard in Flanagan and Weber, op. cit., p. 91. This is more common in dealing with staff unions than with those representing manual workers, according to Gennard. He also reports that Shell (United Kingdom) requires of a union seeking to represent staff employees, that before the company extends recognition (which entails "a ballot of workers"), the union "must produce in writing an undertaking that any other union which has shown interest in recruiting the group concerned will withdraw ...".

[4] David J. Forsyth, "Foreign-Owned Firms and Labour Relations: A Regional Perspective", British Journal of Industrial Relations, Vol. XI, No. 1, March 1973, pp. 27-28, and letter to E.M. Kassalow, ILO, 24 January 1975.

area, after it opened a new plant in 1962, seem to have this origin. The area was largely underdeveloped, working-class traditions were somewhat special and in contrast with older industrialised areas less strong.

Multinational companies entering certain countries in recent years are probably more able than some national companies to take advantage of special tax and other attractions offered by government to locate in such development areas. This may make them a special target in a number of respects.

In the first place the area residents may resent such concessions going to "outsiders". Then, too, the international ties and reputations of such plants may make them appear especially affluent to nationals in the host country. They are also among if not the largest of establishments in such areas.

These factors are likely to make multinationals a particular target of union action, where there is any degree of flexibility in bargaining open to a union.[1] On the other hand, local employers often resent the intrusion of a large outsider into the labour market, and may make efforts to see that the newcomer keeps within the parameters of local wage and other benefits. Together these forces can lend to some union-management conflict. Such has been the experience, as reported by several unionists, with several multinationals in Belgium.

To return to the general problem of the assimilation of multinationals in different regions, Marc Beckers and his collaborators in a study of the social impact of multinationals in Belgium note that as regards "the necessary lapse of time" before which multinationals "conform to regional norms in matters of industrial relations", this varies according to the "integration" of the region. Where a multinational enters an already well-developed region, where the rate of unionisation is high and collective agreements are well established, the multinational is usually likely to adapt to regional norms rather quickly. Although the same authors qualify this by noting that "At the beginning, the largest part of the directors of these [multinational] enterprises are not prepared to enter into the system of industrial relations ...". The strength of the unions quickly brings them into that system in such "integrated" regions.[2]

In less "integrated" regions, where the unions are weaker, the union often has a more difficult path with the "foreign entrepreneurs". Relations are often more "tender" and disputes may occur over fundamental issues of working conditions and work organisation.[3]

Role of union and employer associations in recognition process

Union recognition difficulties among foreign multinational subsidiary firms, or other firms of generally comparable size, in France and Belgium in the industries under study in this report have been conspicuous by their absence. This seems to stem primarily from the fact that in France and Belgium, it is a virtually universal practice for large firms to be members of their appropriate trade or industry association, and recognition is usually extended to unions automatically by such associations. In France, for example, given the social and economic functions and role of the employers' associations, it is extremely difficult for any firms to remain outside of these associations. When this is added to the system of national union representativity[4], it is not surprising that there are no such difficult recognition cases. Much the same is true in Belgium.
----

[1] Forsyth writes that especially in "lagging regions", the "superior ability to pay" of foreign subsidiaries can make them "attractive targets for industrial action". Ibid., p. 27.

[2] Marc Beckers, Jean-Pol Frère, Roger Saucier and Guiseppe P. Torrisi, La Belgique face aux Investissements étrangers, Une Approche sociologique (Louvain, Université de Louvain, 1973), pp. 82-84.

[3] Ibid., pp. 85-86.

[4] See Alan Gladstone and M. Ozaki, "Trade Union Recognition for Collective Bargaining Purposes", International Labour Review, Vol. 112, Nos. 2-3, August-September 1975.

In the Federal Republic of Germany, where so many of the important structures of industrial relations are prescribed by law (works councils, representation on supervisory boards, etc.), labour relations areas in which they might choose to exercise their own options are limited for multinationals.

In Sweden the great strength of the trade unions[1] and the employers' associations makes it difficult for any substantial enterprise, especially a multinational one to "hold out", and with association membership goes union recognition.

In the case of the US electronics engineering company already referred to above (the electronics firm which has withheld union recognition in the United Kingdom and the Netherlands), it began by seeking to avoid union recognition in Sweden, and it remained outside the employers' association. After several decades of operations, it extended union recognition, but remained outside of the employers' association. It found itself pressed hard by its counterpart unions in bargaining at the plant level, sought help from the employers' association, and eventually joined the latter, ending its attempt at an entirely separate relationship. It continues, however, to negotiate separate agreements with its unions, and even though these agreements largely follow the one between the employers' association and the national unions, this separate approach remains exceptional in Sweden.

Another United States engineering firm, this one in the automobile industry, had a somewhat similar experience in the pre Second World War period in Sweden. This company began with a Swedish sales operation in the 1920s and introduced some assembly operations in the thirties. It was asked by the employers' federation to join up shortly after the Second World War as it began to expand its manufacturing operations, and finally did so only in 1957. This same automobile company is not federated in the United Kingdom, and in recent years briefly sought to stay outside the employers' federation in France, but later joined. It was also for many years outside the employers' federation in the Federal Republic of Germany, but joined in the early sixties as it began to feel sharp, direct pressure from the metalworkers' union, which sought to bargain separately and directly with the company.

Multinationals and white-collar unions

The carry over of some US attitudes into Western European industrial relations areas is also revealed in some of the multinational experience with white-collar union recognition. The organisation of white-collar employees in private industry in the United States is much less common than in most of Western Europe. Union and some employers' associations officials in Western Europe indicate that in the earliest stages of their implantation especially, some US companies have more difficulty in accepting such unions than is true of national companies. Unions representing supervisory personnel can present special difficulties for some US companies.

A large white-collar union representing especially higher level technical and supervisory employees in the United Kingdom has complained about "the marked tendency" of US-owned subsidiaries "to be more hostile towards white-collar trade unionism, on the basis that trade union organisation of the staff weakens what is seen as management prerogative".[2] This same insistence on the special difficulties of obtaining recognition at US-owned subsidiaries was also voiced by another representative of this same union when he was interviewed in London.[3]

----

[1] Among manual workers the rate of unionisation is estimated as close to 90 per cent, for non-manuals it is a little lower in Sweden.

[2] Speech of a delegate of the Association of Scientific, Technical and Managerial Staffs, in 1973. See Report of the 105th Annual [British] Trades Union Congress, Blackpool, 3-7 September 1973 (London, 1973), p. 594.

[3] On the other hand Gennard and Steuer, BJIR ..., op. cit., p. 155, state that this problem of non-recognition of staff unionism "is not particularly a symptom of foreign-owned companies since domestic firms have shown a dislike of white-collar unions ...". They add, however, "... Foreign companies have shown a reluctance to recognise staff unions even where they have granted recognition to manual unions without much difficulty. The policy of a number of foreign companies is to have informal contacts with staff union officials but not to grant formal recognition ...".

This white-collar union recognition issue in the United Kingdom may be related, as is the general issue of recognition in some industries in that country, to the general problem of membership in employers' federations. The latter, in some cases, have extended blanket recognition to white-collar along with manual unions, but where multinationals are not association members, they are not likely to recognise white-collar unions "automatically".

The recognition of foremen and cadre unions, groups largely excepted from the usual collective bargaining relationships under US law and custom, can be particularly difficult for some US companies. A US company labour relations officer, in Belgium, expressed his company's difficulties, on this matter, as follows:

... We believe the chef de section (factory foreman) has basic responsibility for managing his human, his technical resources. Because we insist on this involvement and acceptance of responsibility to those who work for him, this has created some differences of opinion with union representatives. We are hopeful that these differences can be worked out - that experience will permit a mutual accommodation satisfactory to both parties ...[1]

Another US company industrial relations executive puts his company's experience with supervisory unions, in the United Kingdom, this way: he observes that its subsidiary in that country "as well as industrial relations practitioners generally, appreciated" the position of his company "in the United States that union representation of its supervisors was neither in their interest nor the company's and, in the United States, the management would adamantly resist such representation ...". However, "after several years of discussions" with the union in the United Kingdom and "after a careful study of what further steps" the company could "take to assure good relations with its supervisors without the intervention of a union", the management "finally decided to extend recognition ...".[2] The affair obviously was something of a difficult policy issue for home company policy makers, even though the general engineering employers' association-union procedures in the United Kingdom provided for the extension of union recognition to these same grades of employees (the company was not a member of the engineering federation).

Several Belgian union officials pointed to cases where, they claimed, management of US subsidiaries made an effort to classify large numbers of cadre and technical groups in such a fashion, that they would be outside of the unions' reach. Their status was described, by the company, as confidential, and for this and related reasons they were claimed, by the company, to be exempt from inclusion in the various plant social elections. Again, it is difficult to say whether this is an attitude which one might find among many Belgian as well as multinational managers, but the multinational cases were singled out by Belgian unionists.

Since multinational companies are often very research and development oriented, and they are also likely to employ the highest, newest technology, they probably employ a greater proportion of technical and cadre personnel. This may make them particular targets of white-collar and technical unions.

In the Netherlands, one union officer indicated greater difficulty in negotiating with US companies on white-collar employees' (especially in the higher ranges) wages, than with Dutch companies. This seemed to result from the fact that a few such companies, at least, had company-wide standards for salaried employees, and any bargaining agreements affecting such employees had to be referred back to the companies' European headquarters.

In a few cases, multinational companies' special salary systems are also held somewhat as confidential material. This, too, was reported as a bargaining problem

----

[1] Paper by J. Ward, on "The International Corporation and Belgian Labour Relations", to a seminar organised at Louvain, 1970.

[2] Paper presented by Robert Copp to Michigan State University Conference on Industrial Relations Problems of Multinational Corporations in Advanced Industrial Societies, East Lansing, November 1974.

by one Dutch union which felt it difficult to negotiate over salaries without a sure sense of the system in question.[1]

In France too, it was reported that especially new multinational firms occasionally have reservations about recognition of white-collar employees, and especially cadres, even though their groups are covered, for instance, by general recognition practices in the engineering industry. They do generally have to adjust, however, to French practices, it was added.

----

[1] The problems arising in connection with multinational companies having their own "special" wage and job classification systems is dealt with below in Chapter IV.

CHAPTER II

MULTINATIONALS AND EMPLOYERS' ASSOCIATIONS

As has already been suggested, most multinationals in Western Europe are members of their "appropriate" employer associations. Indeed, in some countries such membership is almost necessary for large firms. Not to be a member of the employers' association could result in a large company's having no voice in important consultations on government industrial and social policies. In most of these countries the employers' associations are the customary channel for such government-employer exchanges and, in some cases, implement the decisions. One French employer association official commented that given the "dirigiste character of the French economy", non-membership was almost an impossibility, particularly for a firm of any significant size. On the other hand, in the United Kingdom where the system of industrial relations is more voluntaristic, and where a few important British firms are "non-federated", a number of important multinationals are not members of any employers' federation.

Multinationals' role in employers' associations

Managers of foreign multinationals which are members of employers' associations do not usually play a first line role in such associations, i.e. they rarely occupy top officer positions. This seems to be a result of two factors: one is that most multinationals often seek a less conspicuous, less publicly prominent role; and two, the road to the highest posts in employers' associations is frequently by election, and managers from multinationals are not likely to command large votes from national company association members even though this survey found that the managers of multinationals, especially in the personnel and industrial relations sections, are likely to be host country nationals.

In some employers' associations, however, there are special committees composed of the larger companies belonging to the association, and multinationals may have a prominent role in substructures of this type. The existence of such special committees probably is a useful channel for multinationals among other large companies to exercise some of their influence on association policies.

Multinational companies do, in several countries, play a more active and direct role in regional employer association groups, and often it is in these bodies that important industrial relations decisions may be taken. One case is reported in Belgium where two large US engineering firms in one region, the area's most important companies, took the lead in eliminating wage negotiations at that regional level. It was argued that these region-wide wage negotiations were but a preliminary settlement which was almost invariably followed by negotiations at the company level. According to management this made for a kind of double economic jeopardy, especially in the case of large, well-off firms. The same drift toward more company or plant wage bargaining can be observed elsewhere in Belgium.

Non-membership in employers' federations

With the exception of the United Kingdom, there are today virtually no important cases of foreign multinational firms' subsidiaries in the countries and industries studied which are not members of their "appropriate" employers' association. In most of these countries, as for example Belgium, the "national or regional [collective] agreements, negotiated by employers' associations can have a binding effect on all employers, regardless of the fact whether the employer is a member of the employers' association or not".[1] Blanpain adds that this explains, in part, why some of the multinationals join such associations. Without membership they would have no influence at all on the negotiation of agreements affecting them.

----

[1] See Roger Blanpain, "Multinational Corporations as Agents of Change and Innovation in Industrial Relations" - Paper delivered to Michigan State University Conference on Industrial Relations Problems of Multinational Corporations in Advanced Industrial Societies, East Lansing, November 1974.

Looked at in a different light, however, it can be said that one of the most critical aspects of union-management relations, the negotiation of the collective agreement, is, under these conditions, to an important degree out of the direct control of the individual enterprise, and in the hands of the association.[1] This often creates some adjustment difficulties for US multinational firms, which are accustomed to doing their own contract negotiations directly.

One industrial relations executive of a US firm operating in Belgium has noted that with some exceptions in the United States, collective bargaining by "employer associations are not common ...". He contrasts this with his experience in Belgium where employer associations do "the major bargaining" and his company has "little voice in its results" which leaves him "disquieted":

... Our company's experience has been to handle all collective bargaining itself. This naturally builds an attitude of self-reliance and direct participation in a function, the results of which are most important to a company. As we observe collective bargaining in Belgium, we find employer associations ... doing the major bargaining and our company having little voice in its results. We make no case either for or against the system except to state that we sometimes find ourselves disquieted by trends, direction and results of this approach to bargaining.[2]

While this is the experience of only one US subsidiary executive in Belgium, it seems to catch some of the attitude of a number of US companies. This attitude explains, in part, why a number of US companies in the United Kingdom both in the metal trades and the food industries are not "federated", i.e. not members of employers' associations.[3]

Behind this attitude, which is particularly evident in the United Kingdom, lies the fact that industrial relations as a management technique, science or art has often been more highly developed in US firms than those in many other countries. Most larger US companies - and this would embrace multinationals - have elevated the industrial relations function to a higher level in the corporate structure than is the case with many European firms. This also makes the US company more reluctant to delegate the function of contract negotiation.[4] (A similar elevation of the personnel function is also occurring now in a number of large European firms. One can observe a certain symmetry between much of the structure and many of the actions of multiplant and multinational firms.)

The structure of the bargaining process in the United States, with its emphasis upon individual company or occupational units and exclusive single union recognition for such units has also encouraged US firms to develop their own industrial relations capacity. Working to the same end, is the emphasis in the United States, especially in large companies, upon internal, formal company-union grievance procedures. The great size of the US internal market, and the large size of so many firms, also enhances this process. For US firms the subsidiaries implanted abroad may still represent only a relative minority of their business; by contrast for Dutch, Swedish, Swiss and even some British multinationals their subsidiaries abroad may represent the majority of their total business, and adaptation to host country conditions and institutions may come easier.

It is not surprising, therefore, that in the United Kingdom where even a few important national firms are not members of employers' federations, a number of US
----

[1] The right to reject union recognition is also usually removed from a firm's hands when it joins an employers' association in some countries, since membership usually extends recognition. This issue of non-recognition is, in the case of the United Kingdom, discussed below.

[2] Paper by J. Ward "The International Corporation and Belgian Labor Relations", to a seminar organised at Louvain, 1970.

[3] See Gennard and Steuer, BJIR ..., op. cit., p. 1953, for the names of a number of US firms operating in Britain, which are not members of employers' associations.

[4] Steuer and Gennard comparing US and British firms comment: "Domestic firms appear to deploy a smaller amount of management input into industrial relations than the foreign firms, especially the American ones ...". In United States firms "The personnel director is ranked in importance with other specialised functions, e.g. production, research, rules and accountancy ...". See Dunning, op. cit. p. 96.

firms have opted not to join employers' associations. This has, in turn, meant that in the United Kingdom they were not bound by the agreements negotiated by these federations. Some US multinationals have also developed, under these circumstances, their own internal plant grievance procedures to a greater degree than is true of many British firms which usually depend upon the general union-federation procedures.[1]

The feeling of some US firms about conducting their own industrial relations is deep and is attested to by what has occasionally happened during a "takeover" of a British firm by a US-based multinational. In the case of one major US auto producer, the takeover of a large British firm, was followed not long after by the withdrawal of the firm from the Engineering Employers' Federation.[2] The firm in question was, incidentally, choosing the status already enjoyed by the two other major US auto firms in the United Kingdom which were also not federated.

This practice of non-federation in the United Kingdom, it should be added, is only very rarely followed by multinationals from countries other than the United States. Most of these European-based firms are accustomed, in their own countries, to being members of employers' associations which play an important role in industrial relations.

Non-federation and non-recognition of unions

There are, of course, also cases in the United Kingdom where multinationals remained outside of their employers' associations in order "to continue policies of non-union recognition which would be incompatible with association membership ...".[3]

The manner in which the issue of federation or non-federation membership in the employers' association can become a vital labour relations issue was illustrated in the "famous" Roberts-Arundel case in the United Kingdom some years ago.

In this case a US-based firm Roberts, a producer of textile machinery, which had, incidentally, no unions in its US plants, took over the Arundel company in 1965. In the takeover the new firm first continued Arundel's membership in the regional (Manchester) Engineering Employers' Federation (EEF) and with it recognition of the unions.

Beginning a process of rationalisation of Arundel's admittedly run down facilities the company proceeded to lay off some 51 men in late summer 1966. About the same time it closed its plant at Preston (United Kingdom). The company also began to shift some machinery including bringing some of the machines from Preston to Stockport. Some additional changes were introduced to help clean up a somewhat

----

[1] There are cases where a US-based firm has, on occasion, joined its "appropriate" federation, in order to take advantage of the procedures established by that federation and the national unions with which the latter bargains. The Commission on Industrial Relations, in one case in recent years involving Hoover Limited, reported "Both Company and AEF [the union involved in this case] are agreed that the decision of the company to federate was in order to provide management with an external appeal system; they wanted access to senior union officials ...". CIR, Report No. 11, Hoover Limited (HMSO: London, 1970), p. 38. In this case the company was seeking external procedures, unlike the situations of some other multinationals we are describing in this report. The unions had, in general, been critical of this company's earlier reluctance "to invoke external procedure".

[2] According to Duane Kujawa, "one reason" this company left "the Engineering Employers' Federation (EEF) was that it wanted its own management to exercise more direct control over bargaining issues ...". International Labor Relations Management in the Automobile Industry, A Comparative Study of Chrysler, Ford and General Motors (New York, Praeger, 1971), p. 183. There are, of course, also "cases of American-owned firms who have acquired British firms and then joined an employers' association even though the previously owned British firm was not a member ...". Gennard and Steuer, BJIR ..., op. cit., p. 153. The same authors also cite the case of one engineering firm which withdrew from the EEF after being taken over by a Canadian firm. See Steuer and Gennard in Dunning, op. cit., p. 95.

[3] Gennard in Flanagan and Weber, op. cit. p. 91.

cbsolete plant. The company also objected to some of the older "labour" practices, including the system of tea breaks.[1]

As it made production changes, some weeks after the layoff of 51 employees and the closing of the Preston plant which also produced uneasiness among the Stockport employees, the company proceeded to bring in several new women employees to shop-floor jobs. It was the company's contention that these were new jobs; the unions, of course, with the recent memory of the 51 layoffs and the closing of the Preston operations, were suspicious. Moreover, under the Engineering Employers' Federation-Union procedures, there was provision for consultation in advance with the unions[2] when such changes including the introduction of new female jobs were to be made, and this seemed not to have been done.

The regional Engineering Employers' Federation attempted to mediate the dispute. Agreement seemed to be reached that a freeze would be placed upon the further hiring of women workers, the strike would end, and discussions between unions and the management would resume to attempt to resolve the issue. The company continued its claim that the jobs in question were not the old ones, but new ones, and they had the right to hire and move women workers into them. The union continued the strike.

That the company felt unduly bound or constrained by the EEF procedures and agreements seems substantiated by the fact that its next step was to withdraw from the Federation. It also proceeded to advertise in local area papers for 255 men and women, "individuals who appreciate working in a free atmosphere rather than the bureaucratic and restrictive environment of a union shop".[3]

During the strike which stretched on over a year several efforts were made to conciliate the dispute by unions, the Engineering Employers' Federation and government officials. Disagreement over the number of strikers to be rehired and the order of the rehiring, including union insistence on the priority to be accorded to shop stewards in the rehiring made settlement difficult. The unions mounted extensive support from other unions in the general area. Occasional demonstrations at other plants in the area provoked resentment by some employer members of the regional EEF, especially since it was contended Roberts-Arundel was no longer a federation member.

When finally a formula for ending the strike was devoloped by the regional Engineering Employers' Federation office and regional officers of the Amalgamated Engineering Workers Union and seemingly was accepted by local management and unionists, a last minute rejection by the company's United States President, who came to England, frustrated the effort.[4] The final comments of the US firm's President, made after the decision to close down had been taken, reveal the general pathos of the experience, an example of industrial relations at cross-cultural purposes:
----

[1] The company management contended changes were long overdue. "The usual 10-minute tea breaks usually ran to 20 minutes, and every man had his little stool ... some of the old workers had beds in the cellars where they could sometimes sleep ...". The unions claimed the "only beds in that factory were the ones used for fire watching during the war ...". They also charged the company smashed the workers' tea mugs and stools "to force them to use the firm's new vending machines". See The Sun, 3 March 1967. Also see Amalgamated Engineering Union, Roberts-Arundel, The Story of the Strike (no date, presumably 1967).

[2] Not only was Roberts not accustomed to dealing with unions, but it later complained that "the presence of five unions did not make it easy ...". See the article by the American entrepreneur in the case, Mr. Robert Pomeranz, published in the Financial Times, 13 December 1967.

[3] Manchester Evening News, 6 December 1966.

[4] The formula had involved agreement by the local employers' association whose members were willing to guarantee jobs to a substantial number of those on strike for a period of 12 months and thereby relieve Roberts-Arundel of some of the immediate rehiring burden. The head of the association (Manchester Engineering Employers' Federation) bitterly concluded: "I am really disappointed. I am absolutely convinced in my own mind that this firm does not want a settlement ...", the Financial Times, 25 October 1967.

... This is a story of our own lack of experience of British practice, as much as union intransigence. I have made mistakes. Are the unions aware of any they have made? ...[1]

The Roberts-Arundel case is not of course typical of multinationals' labour experience in the United Kingdom. Indeed, it is a relatively small company and its experience rather exceptional. It does, however, illustrate some of the labour problems which can be generated when a foreign company takes up operations in a cultural and industrial relations system which is alien to it.

----

[1] _Financial Times_, 13 December 1967. In May 1968 an agreement between the parties officially terminated the dispute; the unions were recognised but in effect about all that remained was a liquidation and warehouse operation.

CHAPTER III

LABOUR PROBLEMS AND UNION REACTIONS CONNECTED WITH INVESTMENT,
PRODUCTION AND EMPLOYMENT POLICIES OF MULTINATIONALS

It has already been suggested that in Western Europe, most multinationals adapt or conform, to a considerable extent, to national industrial relations systems; however, individual cases of non-conformity to national patterns of multinational companies in one area or another of labour relations are so numerous, that they arouse concern among the unions in almost all countries.

One general area where most unionists at all levels feel keenly that multinational decision-making is not made nationally is in the matter of investments which can vitally effect employment. It is not surprising, therefore, that this is a great source of concern. Here most unionists surveyed were searching for a transnational device or institution or relationship, so that they could have some influence on related investment and employment developments.

Investment decisions, a home office function

It is generally agreed by most management officials as well as by trade unionists that the general investment parameters, i.e. the major decisions to expand or contract - were determined by the home offices of the foreign multinational subsidiary plants in Western Europe. Lest there be confusion, it is not intended to suggest that all subsidiary plants have no input into this process; indeed, the home office of a multinational would scarcely make a decision to increase its investment in a given foreign country without consulting the local subsidiary management, or estimating the related market of the plant in question. Moreover, it is likely that where a given subsidiary plant is selling exclusively, or nearly exclusively in its own host country market, the subsidiary's input into the decision made by the home country managers will be given considerable weight. Thus, for some multinational subsidiaries in the food industry, where exports frequently seem to count for less than may be the case in automobiles or computer parts, the weight of the subsidiary is likely to be greater in this investment decision. On the other hand, if the subsidiary plant in question is only one part of an integrated production chain, or is heavily involved in selling outside the host country, its weight in the investment decision will count for less.

Confusion in the understanding of this process was revealed in one discussion with personnel directors of food manufacturing companies in one of the countries surveyed. Their spokesman was seeking to emphasise the central role of the subsidiary. Of course, he added, "in the case of our own company in a given year we may receive requests for 110 million pounds of new investment funds from subsidiaries around the world. If we have, as might well be the case, only 70 million pounds available, of course the subsidiaries are requested to trim their demands, and finally the centre makes the allocation process". That is the point of course; for major new investments in multinational companies there is inevitably some central allocating function.

Studies in the United States of typical large companies suggest that this finance-investment decision function is perhaps the most critical one to emerge at the top level of giant companies as they evolve. Other decisions such as those which relate to production organisation and marketing, may be parcelled out to divisions or departments but the major decisions on allocating the companies' resources is retained, in the general case, in a very top, central committee.

In a well-known study of the evolution of structure of major industrial enterprises in the United States, Alfred D. Chandler, Jr. notes that in this evolution the division of decision-making between various corporate levels has reached the following point: (1) the managers in "the field unit" are "concerned with one function - marketing, manufacturing, engineering and so forth - in one local area"; (2) executives at the departmental headquarters level "plan, administer, and co-ordinate the activities of one function on a broad, regional and often national scale rather than just locally"; (3) at the next level, "the divisional executives, on the other hand, deal with an industry, rather than a function ..."; (4) "finally executives in the general office have to deal with several industries or one industry in several broad geographical regions ...". And,

Chandler, notes, "They set policies and procedures and allocate resources for divisions carrying out all types of functions ... Their business horizons are broadened to range over national and even international economies." In general, the central allocation function is clearly reserved for the general staff of the company. Again Chandler, in another context, notes that "The executives in the central office ... had to supervise and allocate resources to several business functions ..."[1]

While Chandler's work is on United States corporations, a recent survey of three large British multinationals shows that the allocation of financial resources is similarly done at the "head office" of those companies' organisations. In the case of Unilever, for example, this study notes "... the financial control of the head office is unusually stringent". It adds, "Most of the subsidiaries have to clear their cash position daily through a Unilever account", and "the amounts which even senior field commanders can spend without" the approval of the central control committee "are very modest indeed ...". For example, even in one large important division the chief "cannot approve any item of capital expenditure costing over 100,000 pounds without "the central committee's blessing".[2]

Conversations with various employer association officials also generally bore out the foregoing view of the investment process in multinational companies.[3] In some instances the central allocating function was exercised mainly by setting budget parameters for the subsidiary, with the latter largely free within those parameters. Several union negotiators at multinationals reported that host country plant managers on occasion would indicate their inability to take this or that step because it might overrun their general budget parameters. In many instances the subsidiary had freedom to make modest investment allocations on its own, but the thresholds were usually clearly indicated.

While this survey could not go deeply into the subject, it did appear that where the multinational was in a joint venture with host country interests, the subsidiaries' decision-making power over investment might be more important.

How much further broad company control may go in accompanying the investment process varies greatly. With a highly developed technology, in a refinery, for example, the central office may have some very particular ideas on manning patterns, which it can convey to the subsidiary. With standard-type tobacco manufacturing equipment, or with a fairly standardised automobile operation that has been developed at home, the centre may seek to guide the subsidiary to some effect. On the other hand, with a more labour-intensive product, such as might be the case in the manufacture of some foods or related products, the degree of central control may be low or even non-existent on manning or labour organisation.

----

[1] Alfred D. Chandler, Jr., _Strategy and Structure, Chapters in the History of the Industrial Enterprise_ (Cambridge, Mass: MIT Press, 1969), pp. 12 and 290. Chandler surveys the organisational history of Standard Oil of New Jersey, Dupont, General Motors and Sears Roebuck to illustrate the way in which giant United States corporations have evolved to their present general organisation state and functional divisions.

[2] Graham Turner, _Business in Britain_ (Middlesex, England: Penguin Books, Rev. Edition, 1969), p. 123. Turner's analysis is confined to Unilever, ICI and Shell. A recent report of the British Commission on Industrial Relations, on a Swedish multinational operating in the United Kingdom, notes the general independence of the subsidiary, but that it "is subject to Swedish control on budgetary and technical matters". _Report No. 18, Electrolux Ltd._ (London: HMSO, 1971), p. 2. _The Financial Times_, 12 October 1974, reports a general decision by "Philips, the Dutch electrical group ... to introduce more short-time working at various European manufacturing plants ...".

[3] For a somewhat different view of this analysis of the role of the central home office in the investment process in multinationals, see International Chamber of Commerce, _Realities, Multinational Enterprises Respond on Basic Issues_ (Stockholm, International Chamber of Commerce, 1974). Based on questions submitted to some 25 companies, this survey did not ask directly about the control of the investment function, but it was almost implicit in one question, and a fair minority of companies stressed the role and power of the subsidiaries in their reply. See pp. 30-38.

Investment decisions and union
employment fears

    Some of the investment decisions (more precisely those relating to
disinvestment) are critical from the point of view of employment security. For the
unions, in host countries, the lack of contact with the central office making such
critical investment decisions which can vitally affect employment is nearly
everywhere worrisome and makes for a difficult situation. The feeling that
operations can be closed down "arbitrarily" or reduced without the workers having an
adequate voice was articulated very often by unionists. This was true even, in some
cases, where the company was looked upon generally as a "model employer".

    To repeat, this employment insecurity leads the large majority of unionists
surveyed to a desire to have some transnational relation with their parent
multinational companies. In some cases it was recognised that this could open up
difficulties about inter-union (inter-country) competition over jobs, but this was
generally dismissed in the context that the problem would have to be dealt with in
the broader search for employment security.

    This major investment decision-making process in multinationals was often
contrasted with national companies which could be "gotten at" for meetings and
pressures promptly, when investment decisions threatened job losses. In the case of
national, as opposed to multinational companies, it was also the conviction of a
number of unionists that they could more effectively mobilise the force of their own
governments to help influence company policy on proposed plant closures, layoffs and
the like. Several government as well as a number of union officials indicated a
certain frustration in dealing with some multinational shutdowns, since they were
often not even able to engage the real decision makers in discussion as they were
usually at the central headquarters. Local managers may not have made the decision
to close in the first instance.

Union dealing with shutdown operations
of multinational companies

    In almost all of the countries surveyed, there were several reports or
complaints from union officials and some government officials of precipitous plant
or department shutdowns by multinationals, with little or no notice to the affected
workers, the unions or government officials.

    This seemed to be somewhat less true in the Federal Republic of Germany where
the system of works councils and worker representation on company supervisory boards
provided considerable protection against the possibility of precipitous layoff
actions. Even in the case of the Federal Republic of Germany, however, a top
officer of the food and tobacco workers' union reported to a recent Congress of the
International Union of Food and Allied Workers' Associations, that multinationals
often "do not respect the social legislation ...". He gave as an "example the
actions" of a large tobacco company which "ordered the closing of a plant in
practically one night, bypassing the union and without bothering to consult the
works council ...".[1]

    A number of similar cases were reported in Belgium, the Netherlands and
France, and to some extent the United Kingdom. These cases of fairly precipitous
shutdowns by multinationals were often contrasted with national company situations
where union and governmental pressures might be brought to bear more effectively, at
least to delay if not cancel such closings.[2]

    To some extent the growth of legislation and collective agreement provisions
to improve employment security (the requirement of substantial notice to workers,
and government, before operations can be shut down, substantial termination
----

    [1] IUF, 17e Congrès, Documentation et Procès-Verbaux, Geneva, 23 January-1
February 1973 (Geneva, 1973), p. 22.

    [2] One recent case was cited in France, where a United States auto manufacturing
company announced a forthcoming major layoff, but then withdrew the proposal under
a variety of pressures. The workforce was later trimmed, somewhat by attrition,
offering special severance bonuses, etc. Some of the unionists stated that complex
union relations issues were also involved in this case.

payments, etc.) has been relieving the impact of shutdowns in most of Western
Europe. But aside from strict conformity to the law or to collective agreement
provisions, during interviews in several countries it was stated by a number of
unionists and some other officials (governments and employers) that some United
States multinationals in particular seemed more casual about layoffs or closures
than was the general run of national companies.[1] Cases involving shutdowns by
multinationals home based in Western European countries have also provoked sharp
union reactions in recent years.

Take-overs and subsequent employment losses: union reactions

Especially resented by some union and government officials were instances in
which multinationals had taken over a national (host country) company, and then
later proceeded to shut down all or an important part of its operations, with
consequent layoffs. The belief that the multinational had been permitted entry,
granted the right to takeover a local operation, and then engaged in such shutdowns
engendered a sense of "betrayal" on the part of the unions, and in some cases
government officials. It was readily admitted that in several instances the company
taken over was in poor condition and all or parts of it might have gone under, in
the absence of the takeover; but the multinational is especially expected to be on
its special mettle when it enters a host country.

When, as happened in several important Belgian and Dutch takeovers, a
multinational promises the authorities that there will be no subsequent job
disturbances, and then is unable or unwilling to live up to this promise,
particularly bitter labour relations can develop. It has led to increased
discussions among the unions that there should be certain guarantees demanded by
multinationals proposing to take over national firms. In addition, several unions
have been insisting that they, too, be consulted in any proposed takeovers by
foreign multinationals.

In a 1970 Conference on International Companies, the British Trades Union
Congress adopted "lines of action" which included proposed steps to help control the
social consequences of foreign multinational company takeovers, as follows:

"... 4. To put pressure on the Government ... to ensure that international
firms taking over United Kingdom firms are fully apprised of their industrial
relations responsibilities ... 11. To urge the Government to seek guarantees
of behaviour by international companies investing in the United Kingdom or
taking over United Kingdom firms; guarantees should be subject to sanctions
and should cover: industrial relations practice, manpower plans ..."[2]

----

[1] John Shearer in Barkin et al, op. cit., p. 120, writes: "The uniquely American
casualness about laying off workers causes many difficulties for American firms
abroad, even when they follow scrupulously the severe legal restriction on their
freedom to reduce the workforce ..." Other country multinationals have also been
caught up in strong disputes over the shutdown of operations abroad. There are a
number of articles and books describing the sharp union reactions to the decision of
AKZO, the Dutch-based chemical fibres corporation to close several plants in Western
Europe in 1972. Since this ILO study was largely limited to the food and metal
manufacturing industries, it does not go into the details of the AKZO case.

[2] Trades Union Congress, Report on a Conference ..., 1970, op. cit., pp. 33-34.
An example along somewhat the same lines of ensuring union consultation before
multinationals enter a host country is the statement of the World Confederation of
Labour proposing that unions, at the national level, "demand of the governments and
of the employers legal and conventional measures as well as instruments of control
permitting [inter alia]: the preliminary information of the representatives of the
personnel and of the trade unions before any form of concentration, its reasons,
terms and conditions and probable effects ..." World Confederation of Labour, For
a Policy to Cope with Multinational Companies, September 1973, p. 10. A few
countries have taken steps to impose formal conditions on multinationals which "take
over" domestic firms.

Inter-country transfers and substitutability
of production facilities as a factor in
union-management relations

One of the most serious charges which unions make, from time to time, vis-à-
vis multinational companies is that the latter use their internationally-spread
facilities as a threat to counter union demands and power. If the union will not
yield, the company can or will threaten to transfer its production to another
country, or the company may utilise already existing facilities in another country
to penalise the "demanding" union, or the company may threaten to curtail its future
investments in the country in which the union is making "unreasonable" (in the
company's judgment) demands. All of these tactics are subsumed by the unions under
the general head of threats to shift production as part of the labour tactics of
multinational enterprises.

Typical of union views in this matter are the following:

In many companies the existence of alternative sources of supply gives
management scope to threaten to switch products to other locations. This can
be a very effective bargaining counter. This threat has been made implicitly
or explicitly at Ford's in the last two industrial relations crises.
Production at Dagenham is still substantially larger than in Germany and
Belgium, and a switch of production to the Common Market can sound a very
realistic threat. Similar threats have been made about Vauxhall and Rootes
when industrial disputes are threatened. There is no reason why British-owned
companies should not make similar threats to switch production to Europe. The
means of switching resources over a period of time are considerable. Direct
remittances of profit, the use of royalty and service charges, and the use of
'transfer prices' (pricing intra-company trade at above or below the actual
resource cost) can all be used effectively, and the published accounts of the
company will not reveal any of these items apart from the first. There are of
course national and international regulations on the movement of capital, but
the effectiveness of these controls is open to question. The managements of
international companies thus certainly have the ability to shift the resources
away from areas of high unionisation if this causes them problems. It is of
course exceedingly difficult to discover particular cases where resources have
been switched out of the United Kingdom solely or primarily due to industrial
relations problems. Clearly it is inconceivable that Ford's would close down
their Dagenham site overnight, though the direction of future investment may
well be influenced by industrial relations problems. Given that the effective
life-cycle of capital equipment is well below 10 years in the more advanced
industries, a substantial shift across frontiers can be accomplished in a
relatively short time. Switching investment is the long-term threat. In the
shorter term the impact of internationalised organisation on the collective
bargaining position will depend very much on the nature of the international
company itself. If there are clear alternative sources of supply, then the
management has a much stronger bargaining position in that it can circumvent
the effects of a strike at its United Kingdom plant for some time, assuming
that the United Kingdom plant produces only a small proportion of its total
output.[1]

Similarly, the CGT in France argues:

... the numerous transfers to countries in which wage costs are lower weigh
heavily on general wage levels and undermine the many social benefits which
have often been acquired after many years of struggle by the workers.[2]

The Swedish metalworkers' union comments in a like vein:

Multinational companies have wide opportunities of moving their capital
from one country to another. This makes it more difficult for governments to
pursue an economic policy which pays due attention to the interests of the
citizens of each country concerned. In the same way it makes it more

----

[1] Trades Union Congress, ... Report on a Conference ..., op. cit., p. 11.

[2] CGT, The CGT and the Multinational Companies (Paris, 1973, no page numbers).

difficult for trade union organisations to pursue their demands for higher wages, employment and workers' influence in the firms.[1]

Related to the fear that multinational enterprises can shift production from one country to another, are union concerns that some multinational enterprises are adopting the policy of "dual" sourcing. Under such a policy a multinational enterprise would deliberately seek to have alternative sources of production for given products or components, and thereby reduce the impact of a strike in any one country. The Conference Board, a business research organisation, in its study of multinational unions and companies states, "Some management officials do have such a consideration in mind." It quotes the chairman of the Chrysler Corporation in 1972, who declared, in defence of such sourcing, "'If you do run into a strike situation or a shortage of parts, there may be'" the possibility "'to bring in some parts from another area in order to keep your plant running'".[2]

Obviously such a tactic of dual sourcing is more plausible in some industries than others. For some foods, for example, where government standards prevent the import of many products from abroad which may not satisfy unique national standards, this possibility of dual sourcing may not be as widespread as for electronics or auto parts. But in any case, it is an option more or less unique to the multinational enterprise.

On a somewhat different level is the fear or attitude that is sometimes expressed by unions that a particular operation of a multinational enterprise constitutes so small a part of the company's world-wide operations that it can be treated almost casually. As a consequence the parent company can close down a given subsidiary in reprisal for a strike or what the company deems unreasonable labour conditions. This attitude is somewhat similar to those held by a number of United States unions as a result of trying to bargain in the United States with so-called conglomerate companies whose great variety of holdings similarly render them less vulnerable to action at any one of their many different plants.

A report in the _Financial Times_ on how labour disputes at some motor company plants in Britain were leading one United States company seriously to contemplate the switching of production elsewhere, lends support to the view that where a multinational enterprise's operations are relatively small in a given country, there is a danger it can more easily be closed or phased down:

> "There is a sense in which the United States companies are less deeply committed to the United Kingdom as a manufacturing base; as a proportion of their world-wide operations the United Kingdom is relatively small ..."[3]

The sense of frustration which unions can feel when trying to bargain with but one arm of a many-limbed multinational has been expressed in a report of an official of the International Metalworkers' Federation on his organisation's co-ordination efforts vis-à-vis some of these multinationals:

> 'How effectively can we bargain when we only represent 4 per cent of the company's employees?' That is the question that was put to us at our ITT workers' world meeting last year by the president of the American bakers' union, which represents the workers of ITT's Continental Baking. Of course, this same question is apparent to trade unionists representing workers in the smaller subsidiaries of major multinationals all over the world. Even the powerful unions that represent Vauxhall and Chrysler workers in Great Britain know that they only speak for about 5 per cent in the first case, and a bit of 10 per cent in the second case, of the companies' world workforce.[4]

----

[1] Swedish Metalworkers' Union, _29th Congress, A Programme for Action_, 26 August-1 September 1973, p. 17.

[2] The Conference Board, _The Multinational Union - Challenges the Multinational Company_, Conference Board Report No. 658 (New York, the Conference Board, 1975), p. 3.

[3] The _Financial Times_, 25 October 1973.

[4] Daniel Benedict, "Multinational Companies: Their relations with the workers", report to a Conference on Industrial Relations in the European Community of the Royal Institute of International Affairs, London, 4 October 1973 (Geneva, IMF, mimeographed, 1973), p. 7. The meeting for ITT unions was a joint one which also
(Footnote continued on next page)

This same official took note of the fact that in the very country in which he
was making his address, the United Kingdom, even though the International Telephone
and Telegraph (ITT) subsidiary Standard Telephones and Cables was "quite an
important company ... with some 35,000 employees ..." this was, after all, only 10
per cent of the world employment of ITT. He added, "How much more true is this of
a smaller subsidiary such as Creed and Co. Ltd., which has about 3,000 workers and
less than 1 per cent of the company, or Abbey Life Assurance Co., Ltd, with some 800
workers, or less than one-fourth of 1 per cent of ITT staff ..."

At times, of course, such fears as unions express about the dangers of plant
or department shutdowns or curtailment of future investment as management pressure
tactics may be more in the nature of a psychological reaction, rather than a
physical reality, in the face of bargaining with a multinational company.

Many multinational companies deny "most strongly ... that they can easily
transfer production either temporarily (in the case of a strike) or permanently (as
a retaliatory measure) ...". They argue that "the location and availability of raw
materials, and the cost of transportation ...", the presence of market or tariff
barriers, the variation in production facilities, the time which must be invested to
develop new facilities - the costs of liquidating large investments - these and
other factors would impose an "enormous financial penalty" for any "closure or
reopening of factories" in pursuit of a labour dispute.[1]

While reports of actual production transfers made by multinational enterprises
by way of retaliation or punishment of "recalcitrant" unions are few, there have
been several major "incidents" which tend to reinforce union fears in this regard.
(Aside from other factors, the almost uninterrupted economic expansion in Western
Europe in the decades of the fifties, sixties and early seventies made it unlikely
there would be many instances where multinational enterprises would contemplate
plant shutdowns.) Probably the most well known of these incidents have occured in
the United Kingdom, involving United States auto companies.

Perhaps the single most famous of such "incidents" was the 1971 Ford strike in
Britain.[2] While this dispute was underway early that year, Henry Ford, travelling in
Asia, was reported to have declared that parts of the Ford Escort and Cortina models
which were assembled in Asia would in the future no longer be made in the United
Kingdom but would be manufactured in Asia. In Tokyo, a few days later, Mr. Ford is
said to have remarked, "We cannot remove British exports (to Asia) overnight. It
will be done over a number of years ..."[3]

(Footnote continued from previous page)

involved, among others, the International Union of Food and Allied Workers'
Associations to which the American bakery workers' union is affiliated.

[1] International Organisation of Employers, Multinational Enterprises, the
Reality of their Social Politics and Practices (Geneva, 1974), p. 26.

[2] Even before this "incident" the unions in the United Kingdom were fearful that
because of "difficult" labour relations problems this company might transfer
important operations outside of the United Kingdom, or curtail future investment
there. The International Metalworkers' Federation reported in 1970: "One of those
great multinational corporate decisions made outside of England, Detroit in this
case, which can affect the livelihood of thousands of British workers, may be in the
offing. Escorts which are assembled at Ford's Halewood plant in England, may be
built at a new factory at Saarlouis, Germany. Furthermore only the right-hand drive
version of the TC model, which will replace the Cortina, will be built in Britain.
The Pony, originally intended for manufacture in Britain has already been diverted
to Saarlouis. The company may also decide to make all continental models at the
plant in Germany or Belgium as with the Capri."

"Thus again a big corporation makes decisions on a world scale, concerning
transfer of operations which may enhance company profits but which may also offset
the wellbeing of auto workers in both Germany and England. This is one of the major
problems with which the World Auto Councils are concerned." IMF, News from Sectors
of the Metal Industry, Sector News, No. 5, March 1970.

[3] These comments are quoted from John Mathews, Ford Strike (London: Panther
Books Limited, 1972), p. 137. This 1971 strike resulted from the Ford unions' claim
for "parity" with automobile workers' pay in some of the other major auto companies
in the country.

Mr. Ford came to London shortly thereafter, and in a meeting with (then) British Prime Minister Heath, he is reported to have let it be known, with regard to the company's labour difficulties, that if improvements were not forthcoming, the company would take its business elsewhere.

In this connection, the matter of any future company investments in Britain was raised. The Times of London (16 March 1971) reported Mr. Ford expressed "much dissatisfaction ... with the British [Ford] Company's situation ..." Unless there was "stability over a long period such as three or four years", the Ford Company, which had large overseas investments in view, "could not consider making any new commitments in Britain. Things needed to be cleared up and trade union relations improved ..."

In 1973 when the company decided to locate the bulk of its small car engine production in the United States (for the Pinto model, sold largely in the United States), the Financial Times (22 June) reported:

"It is no secret that industrial disputes in Britain priced the United Kingdom out of this market ..."

The same paper, added, "There was, of course, no guarantee that Britain would ever have been selected for such a major development but the comments of Henry Ford ... [in] the early part of the year made it clear that the United Kingdom had dropped out of the running ..." The same report added, "the fear of similar labour unrest in Germany in the future may have entered into the company" decision to locate the plant in the United States.[1]

More recently, at the Ford Halewood plant in the United Kingdom, which has been involved in several labour disputes, the manger of operations in a letter to the workers indicated that although there existed great European demand for the plant's products, there was the possibility that the company might have to "create manufacturing facilities elsewhere ...":

"If the Halewood workers throw away the opportunity by not meeting high quality standards or by failure to meet schedules, the size of the Halewood labour force is bound to contract because of the company's need to create manufacturing facilities elsewhere".[2]

The refusal of the unions to relax "strict rules on overtime scheduling", has been cited by the Ford Company as a reason why it might "shun Belgium for future expansion".[3]

Difficult labour disputes at the Chrysler plants in the United Kingdom in 1973, provoked somewhat similar overtones or visions of production transfers out of the country, or future reductions of company investment in the country. The Economist commented in June, during the course of one of these disputes, that Chrysler's warning to the workers was "stronger in terms than Henry Ford II's warning in the 1971 strike ...".

Chrysler United Kingdom said on Wednesday what every other car manufacturer would like to say but refrains for reasons of tact: it told its men there would be no more investment until they showed over a reasonable period that they could sort out their differences with the management. Union men and shop stewards expressed shock and horror at this break with good manners. The threat, stronger in its terms than Mr. Henry Ford II's warning in the 1971 strike, arises from a dispute with 300 workers that has so far cost the company £4 million in lost output.[4]
----

[1] It also seems likely that changes in the United States exchange rate as well as accelerating wage increases in Western Europe influenced the decision.

[2] The Financial Times, 21 April 1975.

[3] Wall Street Journal, 28 August 1973, quoting Ford President Leo A. Iacocca.

[4] The Economist, 9 June 1973. The Wall Street Journal of 22 June 1973, carried a story that "The Future of Auto Industry in Britain is Seen Hurt by Bitter Strike at Chrysler Plant". It took note of the statement by the "chief executive of Chrysler United Kingdom", that the company's "'disastrous record of stop-go production caused by industrial disputes and [he] warned there would be no further
(Footnote continued on next page)

Later in 1973, when another labour dispute erupted, the Financial Times reported the Chrysler company threatening to "dismiss" 6,000 workers, "unless the current labour troubles are solved". This was true even though the journal observed Chrysler had made certain "commitments" as regards employment, when it had taken on the British Rootes motor company a few years earlier. The same paper noted Chrysler's withdrawal of United Kingdom built cars from the United States export market also seemed hard to reconcile with that agreement; but the company had to pay its way, the paper warned, and if Rootes had not been taken over, it might have gone under.[1]

More seriously, the Financial Times also observed the labour disputes at Chrysler were currently leading company planners to consider switching substantial production to its French (Simca) plants, and/or to a partner operation in Japan. Where a multinational enterprise has duplicate or similar facilities in other countries, labour problems can take on a very special coloration as the Financial Times report suggests:

> If Chrysler United Kingdom were a purely British concern, the reduction in labour and corresponding rundown in output which the plan [under consideration] implies would be self defeating. But it is no longer a purely British company, and it would be simple for Chrysler to reallocate export markets either to Simca or to its Japanese affiliate Mitsubishi to take up any slack caused by British decline.[2]

The Italian unions, in 1972, bitterly protested the proposed shutdown and presumed transfer of certain operations of the Zanussi Electrical Appliance group to the Federal Republic of Germany. Apparently these transfers were part of a move involving AEG-Telefunken, a company based in the Federal Republic of Germany, which had a large holding in Zanussi. The Italian unions enlisted the assistance of the German metal union (IG Metall) and the European Metalworkers Federation in their campaign against the transfer.[3]

In all of these (and other) cases, it is often impossible to judge if genuine transfers of production followed in the wake of difficult labour disputes.[4] But it is clear, as the Financial Times noted in the Chrysler case, that there are options open to some multinationals which are not open to producers which are entirely home based. It is these options, as well as the occasional reported incident, that help explain the concern of unions in their relations with multinational enterprises.

In any event such production transfers can more easily be effected (or even contemplated!) in some industries or factories than others. Thus, in Western Europe for the most part the output of food products multinational enterprise plants are destined for and in some ways limited to the national markets in which they are produced. Special local standards and regulations make it difficult, if not impossible to sell many types of food products across country lines. But even here, some European unionists cite certain packaged and processed foods which do enter into inter-country trade, and they also relate a few cases where the existence of duplicate facilities of a multinational enterprise in different countries is a potential threat in a labour dispute. The transfer of fish processing operations from the Netherlands plant of a large multinational enterprise to the same company's plant in the Federal Republic of Germany was cited by unionists in both countries, but no labour dispute had been involved. In some instances soap powder production,

----
(Footnote continued from previous page)

capital investments until the present dispute' was resolved". The Wall Street Journal article went on to note the considerable national resentment which was aroused by such a threat from a foreign-owned enterprise.

[1] The Financial Times, 25 October 1973.

[2] The Financial Times, 26 October 1973.

[3] The Financial Times, 20 September and 11 November 1972.

[4] Writing on this subject of production transfers and labour disputes some years ago, the research director of the British Trades Union Congress, David Lea, commented "... This type of threat is quite common as a bargaining tactic in the United Kingdom motor industry, for example, but it is difficult to trace a case where a multinational has closed down or cut back its United Kingdom operations for this reason alone ..." Dunning, Editor, op. cit. p. 152.

produced by some multinational enterprises seemed to be moving from one country to another. Some cases were also cited where margarine was shipped from one country to another, by multinationals, in the course of labour disputes which interrupted production. Multinational food companies cite brand name differences, packaging problems and national standards and regulations as effective barriers to such shifts.

Officials of unions of technicians in France and the United Kingdom technician unionists complained about the policy of some multinational enterprises of transferring research projects and sometimes the personnel engaged therein to other countries. It was alleged that such transfers usually do not involve any great shift of substantial production facilities, and can therefore be undertaken fairly readily by some companies.

Multi-country facilities and
special union tactics

While the existence of multinationals' transnational production facilities in different countries are often cited as a threat to national union power, there are also undoubtedly cases where the extension of facilities beyond national boundaries can make a company more vulnerable than a purely national competitor. As the British Trades Union Congress has suggested, if a "corporation is highly integrated with specialised functions being carried out in different countries ..." a strike in a particular "United Kingdom plant would have an impact on the company's world-wide operations ...".[1]

The International Metalworkers' Federation, for one, has explicitly noted this possibility of transnational company vulnerability at particular production points. In 1973 meetings of its Ford and General Motors affiliated unions in Western Europe, there was discussion of the "key" character of new, specialised transmission plants of those companies in France, and how transnational union strategy might be adapted vis-à-vis these particular plants. Both the General Motors and Ford plants in France were designed to supply certain types of transmissions for virtually all of the European assembly plants of these two companies.[2]

On a different level, multinational companies in the same industry may vary considerably in their degree of integration. The automobile co-ordinator of the International Metalworkers' Federation (IMF) in a 1973 report referred to "a company like Ford" which was in a position "to turn out Cortina and Escort models normally produced at" its plants in the United Kingdom "on its assembly lines at Saarlouis or Cologne in the Federal Republic of Germany", thereby "posing a prime problem for the unions organised in Ford's European operations".

This contrasted, he went on to add, with "General Motors' policy to date of maintaining independent operation of plant units, for example between the British Vauxhall or German Opel". He concluded this could call for varying strategies by IMF and its affiliates vis-à-vis these two companies.[3]

The European operations of Ford are reputed to be more fully integrated than those of General Motors, in other respects. Thus, aside from any duplication of

----

[1] Trades Union Congress, Report on a Conference ..., 1970, op. cit., p. 12. A well-known British writer on multinationals similarly comments, "... The more companies rationalise their production processes so that their operations in different countries become increasingly interdependent, the greater the unions' ability to dislocate their operations will become." Christopher Tugendhat, The Multinational (London, Eyre and Spottiswoode, 1971), p. 180.

[2] E.M. Kassalow, The International Metalworkers' Federation and the Multinational Automobile Companies: A Study in Transnational Unionism, 1974 (mimeographed: to be published later), p. 294 et seq for a description of these meetings.

[3] Ibid., pp. 278-279.

assembly lines, there is a far greater dependence, in Ford, upon trade between specialised parts producers in one country and assemblers in another country.[1]

All of these factors may help explain why Ford tends to account for such a relatively large share of the International Metalworkers' Federation's efforts in the automobile field.

Under some exceptional circumstances unions may be in a position to hinder transfer of operations from their own country to another. Such seems, for example, to have been the case in the Volkswagen Company of the Federal Republic of Germany in recent years. According to a series of newspaper reports, top management has been anxious to begin assembling operations in the United States in order to serve more effectively that important market of the company. Workers' representatives on the Board of VW have tended to view with reserve such a company move. Within the union there have been some fears that this would result in a job loss in the home plants of the company.[2]

As in most cases involving substantial new investment, a variety of factors and forces are doubtless influencing any ultimate decision to locate in the United States or not. Some people contend that a decision not to invest in the United States could lead to more job losses in the Federal Republic of Germany than if a decision to make the investment there was accepted. Their argument is that without assembly operations in the United States, the company might lose more and more of its market there, with ultimately greater job losses at home. Most recently the workers' position seems to have been modified somewhat, particularly in the light cf indications received from new top management in VW that any operation in the United States might only be in the form of some sort of joint venture, for assembly purposes, with a United States auto firm.

In both these cases labour disputes in the Federal Republic of Germany were not at issue, and the move and contemplated move seem motivated by cost and marketing considerations. This option of influencing high level company decisions is, of course, not open to unions in most home country cases, since effective representation on top company levels remains the exception rather than the rule. In any event, the prime concern of this report is with labour relations problems in multinational subsidiaries in the host countries.

————————

————————

[1] See Graham Turner, _Business in Britain_ (Middlesex, England: Penguin Books, 1971), p. 426. Turner writes that "Vauxhall has stated quite categorically that its parent, General Motors, will not follow Ford down the road which leads to a completely integrated European operation".

[2] Financial journals and other newspapers have carried numerous stories on this intra-company discussion from 1973 onward.

CHAPTER IV

MULTINATIONAL HOME OFFICE INTERVENTION:
SOME SECTORS, INFLUENCES AND COUNTRIES

Even where multinational home offices are prone to exercise influence over
subsidiaries' labour practices, this is done more in the case of certain selected
labour "areas" than for others. Whether or not multinational enterprises are prone
to influence subsidiaries' labour policies is also affected by technological and
market forces. Finally, multinational home office propensity to intervene and the
impact of such intervention varies to some extent from country to country.

Technological and market factors influencing home
country involvement in subsidiary labour practices

For multinationals the propensity to intervene or not in their subsidiaries
seems to vary somewhat according to "technological" factors. Thus the likelihood
that home office management may seek to influence an overseas subsidiary plant, or
wish to be closely informed about labour developments at the subsidiary, is greater
if the subsidiary plant in question is a vital part of an integrated production
system, a system which could be widely disturbed if this particular "key" plant was
shut down. Several of those interviewed from both unions and management in the
United Kingdom referred to an important case of a subsidiary plant producing engines
for the company's subsidiaries throughout Europe. The progress of labour relations
or any strike threats in that engine plant were apparently very closely monitored by
the company's home office - more so, apparently, than was the case of most of its
other overseas plants.

"Technological" factors similarly also seem to help explain the fact that
multinational food manufacturing companies seem to "lean" on their overseas'
subsidiaries more rarely than do, to cite a somewhat apposite case, automobile
companies. In the latter industry production systems are more likely to be
integrated, with parts or components being exported from one country to another and
the result may be that strikes or threats of strikes are of greater concern to home
offices. The generally more standard technology of the automobile industry with its
heavy investment requirements, regardless of where any particular plant is located,
may also lead home office management to offer more advice and to supervise
subsidiaries more closely. One petroleum home office executive indicated that he
had a fairly good idea of what manning requirements should be for a given standard
installation, and, therefore, the home office tended to monitor the manning
practices of overseas subsidiaries operating such installations.

B.C. Roberts has pointed to a number of technological variables which can lead
to different responses on the part of multinational enterprises. Thus,
manufacturing companies, for example, are "much less locked in than oil, mining or
tropical product companies". This gives them much greater choice "in whether and
where they manufacture overseas" and this flexibility can "be an important factor in
their relations with host countries", and "it will have an important bearing on"
their "organisation and pattern of industrial relations".[1]

Marketing considerations may similarly influence multinationals in their
policy toward overseas subsidiaries. If, for example, at least an important part of
the output of a particular subsidiary plant is destined for overseas markets, the
home office is likely to be more concerned than if any strike will effect only the
market in which the plant is located.

Whether or not the home country market of the multinational is very large, in
porportion to its total sales, may influence its general policies towards overseas
subsidiaries. For many United States based multinationals the home market share of
the company's total output is likely to be much greater, proportionally, than would
be the case of multinationals home based in Sweden, the Netherlands or Switzerland.
Where the overseas share is relatively small, the home office may tend to regard
overseas problems, including some labour problems, as a mere extension of home
ccuntry operations, and to try to impose home country standards.
----

[1] See his chapter in Hans Günter, editor Transnational Industrial Relations
(London, Macmillan, 1972).

Trying to distinguish those factors which make some multinational enterprises "centrist" and some "non-centrist" one student of United States management concludes that "The size of the home market is probably the more important factor." Thus, those "companies with a large home market tend to be centrist, while those with a small home market tend to be non-centrist". He notes, that a "company with a small home market in Europe" realises "that it must take risks to grow into a world leader ...". This, however, "is not the reaction of an American company that dominates its large home market and is already a world leader by virtue of the volume of United States sales alone".[1]

This influence of market factors on the labour policies of many United States based multinational enterprises was specifically alluded to in an OECD trade union seminar held in 1970. Among the general conclusions of the report of this meeting was that, so far as Western Europe was concerned, the speed with which multinationals adapt to labour conditions abroad "may be influenced by the importance of the foreign activity to the parent company ...". United States firms were said to "differ, say, from Swedish firms" since "seldom more than a small part of total activity" of the former were overseas. In the case of Swedish multinational companies, the bulk of their activities were usually overseas, and they would be more adaptable to labour conditions abroad, since "they are particularly concerned to avoid any major industrial difficulties which might jeopardise total production and total profits".[2]

Multinational company impacts greater in certain countries

This report has already cited instances where multinational enterprises diverged to some degree from local labour practices. When one turns to the question of their general impact on the particular countries surveyed, the evidence is more difficult to find or assess.

The structure of labour relations systems in particular countries makes them more or less pliable to the impact of multinational corporations. For example, the more voluntaristic nature of the industrial relations system of the United Kingdom is likely to allow greater scope for multinationals to introduce some of their own practices as compared to a country like the Federal Republic of Germany where more of the industrial relations systems is laid down in law. The section on employers' associations (see above, Chapter II) has already indicated how the role and strength of these bodies may limit the flexibility open to multinationals. To a degree the same is true of the strength of the union movement; thus, to repeat, in Sweden where the rate of unionisation is very high and a firm relationship exists between unions and employer associations, any scope for multinationals to introduce their own labour practices would also be more limited.

There have been few serious studies of the impact of multinationals on industrial relations in particular countries. Those of Gennard and Steuer indicate a few "areas" where the practices of multinationals have had some noticeable general labour impact in the United Kingdom.

The introduction of "productivity bargaining" is one such case in point. This came about largely as a result of influence "from Foreign-owned firms, particularly Esso, Alcan, Mobil Oil and Shell ...".[3] A study of "Recent collective bargaining trends in the United Kingdom" cites especially the Esso productivity agreement with a series of United Kingdom unions. Under this agreement covering the United States based company's refinery at Fawley, the management "was able to persuade workers to lift restrictions on manning ratios and to accept a great degree of flexibility in the way in which work was carried out". In return the company agreed "to

----

[1] David Gestetner, "Strategy in Managing International Sales", Harvard Business Review, September-October 1974, p. 107.

[2] OECD: Report on the Meeting of Trade Union Experts on Multinational Companies (Paris, 1970), pp. 8-9.

[3] Steuer and Gennard, in Dunning, op. cit., p. 110.

substantially higher rates of pay and other improvements in the terms of employment".[1]

This union-management type of productivity agreement became widely generalised in the country, especially after the establishement in 1965 of a National Board for Prices and Incomes. The Government encouraged unions and managements "to negotiate productivity agreements, since the promise of achieving above-average increases in output was accepted as a justification for above-norm pay increases". Between 1 January 1967 and 31 December 1969, some 5,185 productivity agreements were registered with the Governemnt.[2]

Any other influence of multinational companies in the United Kingdom has been less pervasive than was the productivity agreement. United States companies in the automobile industry, most notably Ford and General Motors, but also later Chrysler (after its take-over of the Rootes Company in 1967), did pioneer with a fixed hourly wage system (along with measured day work, another innovation) in an industry which was very largely devoted to piece-rates or payment by results. The success of the United States companies with such systems as well as technological changes in the industry including the increased utilisation of automated equipment seem to be leading other companies in the same industry similarly to eliminate payment by result.

The tendency of a number of United States owned subsidiaries in the United Kingdom to choose and develop plant or company rather than association bargaining, as well as the practice of some United States subsidiaries to press for fixed term agreements as opposed to the more usual British practice of open-ended agreements does not seem to have had any decisive influence on the country's industrial relations patterns. There does appear now to be some general trend away from association bargaining in the British engineering industry where it has long been practised.

The only other country in this survey, for which a study comparable to those of Gennard and Steuer seems to have been made is Belgium. Summarising that study R. Blanpain indicates that in "integrated regions"[3] most multinational firms were compelled to accept the Belgian industrial relations system. In less integrated regions this acceptance was a slower process. While he cites a number of specific instances in which multinational enterprises diverged from specific national or local labour practices, Blanpain does not indicate any major general changes which could be attributed to multinationals.[4]

United States automobile companies in Belgium have departed on some important occasions from national trends or practices in their general collective bargaining; for instance, General Motors in the late 1950s introduced a three-year agreement at Antwerp, much more in keeping with its United States experience than Belgium's, where shorter-term agreements have been more common in metals. Ford insisted, over strong union opposition, on a five-year agreement at its Genk plant in 1962. These longer-term agreement practices did not become generalised. Both companies, too, seem to have been somewhat in the lead with time rate wages in the automobile industry, but this is less clear than in the case of the United Kingdom.

Strikes and home office involvement

The research of Professor David Blake suggests that the home offices of United States based multinational enterprises are more likely to involve themselves with subsidiaries when it comes to "strike settlements" than in other phases of labour relations. (Some 60 per cent of the respondents to a questionnaire which Blake sent

----

[1] B.C. Roberts and Sheila Rothwell, in International Labour Office, Collective Bargaining in Industrialised Market Economies (Geneva, ILO, 1973), p. 365.

[2] Ibid., pp. 365-366. The authors stress that by then "the concept of a productivity agreement had been greatly broadened to cover almost any change in work practice, hours of work, wage structure and methods of payment".

[3] See above Chapter I for discussion of integrated and less integrated regions.

[4] Blanpain, op. cit. Blanpain leans heavily on the work of Beckers et al, op. cit., in assessing the impact of multinationals in Belgium.

to multinational enterprises replied that headquarters was likely to intervene "frequently" or "sometimes" in "strike settlement" cases). Blake's finding contrasts with that of B.C. Roberts and Jonathan May who submitted a questionnaire similar to that prepared by Blake to a number of British-based multinational enterprises.[1]

Duane Kujawa in his study of the three major United States automobile companies writes, on the question of strikes as regards Chrysler: "In both Canada and Europe, the vice-president of the United States and Canadian automotive group, and the vice-president of the European operations are advised on strikes in their respective areas", and they "approve of local management positions on critical issues". In Ford, the overseas labour liaison manager is informed when a strike occurs at a plant overseas, and "he may participate in activities to settle strikes if local management requests that he do so". Generally, "these requests are made by Ford's smaller affiliates ...". The company's central labour staff "does not specifically approve local management's positions on strike issues ...". At General Motors the central office is "immediately advised whenever a strike occurs at an overseas subsidiary ...". Executives at the central office "offer suggestions to resolve strike issues when called upon to do so by subsidiary management ...". But the central office "does not formally approve local management positions on strikes or actual strike settlements ...".[2]

Aside from the results of any questionnaire research, a number of unions and several management officials interviewed during the ILO survey expressed the opinion that home country involvement in labour affairs of a subsidiary tended to rise when a strike or the threat of a strike occurred. This was particularly true when the strike was _not_ part of a conflict between the host country employers' association and the union (or unions). Thus, any special strike characterisitcs of multinational enterprises are more likely to "show" in countries like the United Kingdom or Belgium where considerable bargaining occurs at the plant or company level, than in the Federal Republic of Germany or Sweden where the unions more critical bargaining takes place with employers' associations.

In one country, Belgium, several United States based multinationals have in the past had what unionists regard as "special" strike experiences. During a strike in 1974 at a large electrical-electronics company, the management retaliated to the unions' tactics by "resorting to tough and total lockout". So rare are "lockouts"

----

[1] David Blake "Cross National Co-operation Strategies", in Kurt P. Tudyka, _Multinational Corporations and Labour Unions_, Selected Papers from a Symposium in Nymegen, 17-19 May 1973 (in processed form), p. 242. B.C. Roberts and Jonathan May, "The Response of Multinational Corporations to International Trade Union Pressures", _British Journal of Industrial Relations_, Vol. XII, No. 3, November 1974, p. 405. A new survey of multinational enterprises, again based on questionnaires, seems to find a far greater degree of centralisation in labour policy than do either the Blake or Roberts-May studies, but it is based on different questions. See the Conference Board, _The Multinational Union Challenges the Multinational Company_, Conference Board Report No. 658 (New York: the Conference Board, 1975), p. 13. The Board also finds that United States based multinationals have more centralised labour policies than do multinationals based elsewhere. These various questionnaire surveys are quite useful in evaluating some aspects of multinational operations; but some of their findings are occasionally difficult to evaluate fully. Take for example the case of a multinational enterprise with 25 plants overseas, and suppose, for illustration, 22 of these plants were part of employer association-union bargaining and collective agreements including wages: in these cases the home office, therefore, had little special influence on the 22 subsidiaries. Let us further suppose that in the three countries where the subsidiary plants bargained directly with "their own" unions, the home office monitored and passed on wage settlements. Just how would a multinational enterprise answer a question on whether it had any role in wage bargaining by its subsidiaries? The same problem presents itself in strikes and other issues. Of course more detailed questionnaires can get at these questions plant by plant, or by groups of plants, where possible; but for most of the general questionnaire surveys published to date, this is not indicated in the results.

[2] Kujawa, op. cit., pp. 58, 116 and 171.

in Belgium that, as one report puts it, there is almost no "clear legal precedent" on which to judge it.[1]

Some years ago in another strike situation, multinational management - in what was quite unusual for Belgium - made strong efforts to clear the path for workers who did not observe the strike, and to operate the plant. The management charged the unions with interfering with free access to the plant.

At several Belgian subsidiaries particular difficulties were reported over management treatment of shop stewards in ways which trade unionists felt were "foreign" in nature. The discharge of union stewards led to strikes in a few cases in subsidiaries of multinational enterprises.

It is sometimes difficult for United States companies in Belgium (and in some other West European countries) to adjust to the fact that the resort to strike is relatively freer, with less definition of rights and responsibilities than is the case of strikes in the United States. One executive of a United States based subsidiary in Belgium commented on this as follows:

In an area of social legislation, we find what could possibly be considered as a paradox. When we examine the great detail and precision ... of the legislation existing in, for example, safety and hygiene, one might assume similar detail in other areas. A notable exception concerns laws relating to strikes. Here there is little or no legislation or "common laws" which serve to define the rights and responsibilities of the parties. We find the absence of such legislation leaves an important area largely undefined and somewhat undisciplined ...[2]

While little or no research has been done on the subject, in several countries a number of unions and a few management officials were inclined to describe personnel managers in subsidiaries of United States multinationals as somewhat "harder" and more inclined to insist on the sanctity of principles in negotiations than might be the case with national companies. This, in turn, may lead to more difficult strikes, when strikes occur.

So far as United States multinational companies are concerned this adherence to principles is probably attributable, in part, to their more highly developed industrial relations functions, or departments, when compared to most companies elsewhere. The United States tradition of individual company bargaining, the more widely voiced doctrine of "management prerogatives" in United States industrial relations, plus the legal and contractual restrictions on the right to strike during the life of an agreement, also enhances this emphasis upon "principles".

During the present survey a Belgian union official stated that "the good number of conflicts in American enterprises were due to their lack of flexibility" in adapting to Belgian "social conditions". He added these enterprises sometimes have "too great a tendency to hold to principles" taken from the United States.[3]

A study of labour relations in the British motor car industry observed of one United States firm that it has been "outstanding" in its disputes "over disagreements about management questions" and the company experiences "frequent strikes on individual dismissals ...". In general wage negotiations, on the other hand, this same company has no special, distinguishing experience.[4]

John Gennard noting the "larger proportion of disputes" in foreign owned subsidiaries in the United Kingdom over "the employment or discharge of particular

----

[1] *Industrial Relations Europe*, Newsletter, June 1974, No. 19, Vol. 1 (Brussels, Management Counsellors Iternational), p. 1.

[2] Paper presented by J. Ward on "The International Corporation and Belgian Labour Relations", to a seminar organised at Louvain, 1970.

[3] Information furnished by letter, dated 14 February 1975.

[4] H.A. Turner, G. Clack and G. Roberts, *Labour Relations in the Motor Industry, A Study of Industrial Unrest and an International Comparison* (London, George Allen and Unwin, Ltd., 1967), p. 243.

employees", believes "that foreign owned subsidiaries have been more inclined to resist union encroachment on managerial 'rights' to hire and fire".[1]

Home office intervention in pensions

There was general consensus, as a report in a 1970 OECD trade union meeting concluded, that multinational enterprises "often provide better finge benefits than domestic companies ...".[2] The report of the International Organisation of Employers on multinationals states that these companies "are certainly at the top" as regards fringe benefits, and "especially as regards pensions".[3]

The same 1970 trade union meeting also concluded that there is a much "stronger tendency" for managerial philosophy of multinational enterprises "to repeat itself [abroad] in fringe benefits, than in, say wage benefits ...". Fringes more often reflect company "philosophy" in this respect, and "It is usual to find a uniform [company] personnel policy which draws together various benefits in a coherent whole."[4]

It is not surprising to find that there is rather widespread agreement that bargaining over pensions (or pension-type benefits) where it takes place was one area where central office participation tended to be high. This was true even in the case of certain countries where trade unionists agreed that there was a high degree of decentralisation as regards labour policy of multinational enterprises. These same unions found that subsidiaries generally had to consult home offices before making significant changes in company pension systems. Similar comments were made in virtually all the countries surveyed. It was noted, however, that some recent changes in pension laws, as for example in the Federal Republic of Germany, were narrowing the scope for separate company pension action.

The IOE survey of responses to its questionnaire on labour practices of multinational enterprises states that unlike "such matters as wages, fringe benefits and other conditions" where power is generally delegated to the subsidiary, "company pensions (supplementing in some cases the national scheme) were mentioned frequently as being administered or controlled centrally".[5]

Duane Kujawa's survey of overseas labour practices of major United States auto companies finds that for Ford, headquarters "labour relations staff approval is required when a subsidiary negotiates major changes in its ... funded benefit programmes ...". At the General Motors Belgian subsidiary, although the "local company decided when a new" pension programme "is necessary", the home office "director of employee benefits has responsibility for the actual preparation of any

----

[1] Gennard in Flanagan and Weber, op. cit., p. 84. This seems to contrast with the earlier report of Gennard and Steuer ... BJIR ... op. cit., p. 158, that there seemed to be nothing very distinguishing about multinational enterprises strikes, and that they might even appear to be "less in magnitude" than in domestic firms. In correspondence with the ILO (30 January 1975) Gennard notes that the problem of "Disputes over Employment or Discharge of Workers ... was not mentioned in the British Journal of Industrial Relations article ... because at the time our interest was mostly with wage matters ...". He adds, in the same letter, that these differences between the foreign-owned sector and domestic firms seem to be diminishing over time. Forsyth, op. cit. (also BJIR), p. 20, taking issue somewhat with the earlier Gennard and Steuer article, concludes that "the United States owned sector in Scotland is shown to be characterised by a much heavier incidence of strike activity than in the indigenous sector ...". Forsyth notes that his sample, in contrast to that of Gennard and Steuer was limited to United States based multinational enterprises.

[2] OECD, Report on the Meeting of Trade Union Experts on Multinational Companies (Paris: 1970, mimeographed), p. 16. The report does add, "this is particularly true in developing countries".

[3] IOE, op. cit., p. 16.

[4] OECD, ... Trade Union Experts ... op. cit., p. 16.

[5] IOE, op. cit., p. 9.

- 32 -

new plan" and it is "ultimately approved by the appropriate committee of the United States parent corporation".[1]

Several labour officers of multinational enterprises indicated there were, in the central home office, pension and/or actuarial specialists who were consulted before significant changes were made in subsidiary pension plans. The critical factor seems to be the long-run financial commitments which pension plans entail and for this reason home offices often insist on being involved to some degree in these commitments.

Special company pensions, generally supplementing national social security systems, have been one of the particular marks of many multinational enterprises in Western Europe. It was widely commented in the ILO survey, however, that important legislative improvements in national social security retirement systems were reducing the role of such private company plans in several countries. Indeed, such improvements in social security systems are tending to reduce the relative importance of nearly all company fringe benefits, not just pensions in most West European countries. It is likely, however, that they continue to be of more stand-out importance in less developed countries.

Multinational companies' wage and job systems[2]

The present survey and others indicate that in the countries studied, wage levels in multinational enterprises are generally established in keeping with national and local labour market conditions and institutions. This is particularly true for manual (blue collar) workers. As has been observed earlier in this report, multinational subsidiaries frequently operate within established budgetary parameters, and these can of course have an influence upon their wage policies.

So far as wage systems, as opposed to wage levels, are concerned it is, however, fairly common in most of these countries for subsidiaries to introduce large or small parts of their own (home country) job evaluation, job rating and other wage system practices. Quite germane to this point is the finding of the British Trades Union Congress in 1970, that while on the one hand "wage negotiations are invariably conducted at a decentralised level" in multinational subsidiaries, this same "decentralisation does not necessarily apply to company policy guidelines or procedure agreements and wage systems ...". In the latter, the TUC found that "there may be a strong degree of centralisation".[3]

It need scarcely be added that there is considerable variation between companies and to some extent countries as to the degree of exportation by multinationals of such wage system practices. There were, however, in every country surveyed at least some important examples cited wherein job evaluation systems, merit rating plans, and the like were imported in large or small part by multinationals.

United States multinationals were particularly noted as the leaders in this regard. Many union and employer representatives expressed the view that United States companies often had more "highly developed and more structured wage and job systems". In two countries, management spokesmen suggested that the importation of important parts of such systems may have been due to the need on the part of distant home offices to establish some sense of control over their widely scattered operations. Moreover, since multinational enterprises generally make use of the most advanced technology, this too may have an influence on their wage structure and systems.

Even beyond the multinational subsidiaries themselves it was suggested that the United States wage and job systems had also had some influence in several
----

[1] Kujawa, op. cit., pp. 112 and 168.

[2] For an analysis of wage levels, see, ILO, Wages and Working Conditions in Multinational Enterprises (Geneva, 1975).

[3] "International Companies and Trade Union Interest", excerpts from the British "TUC Economic Review", in ICFTU, Economic and Social Bulletin, May-June 1970, p. 5. The TUC cited specific multinationals within which "wage payment systems are standardised".

countries on national companies practices. This sometimes came about by imitation or through the recruitment by national companies of managers with experience at United States subsidiaries; sometimes it was attributed to the influence of United States industrial engineering companies.[1] Graham Turner, in his study of three major British companies notes that each of the three, "in recent years ... has gone through a major reorganisation; and all three have brought in McKinsey to help them ...". McKinsey and Company is a leading United States based managerial consulting firm.[2] Similar experiences with United States engineering and managerial firms were referred to in the Federal Republic of Germany.

It has already been observed that there is considerable variation between countries in the matter of job system importation. Dutch union and employer representatives stated that any such external influences had been somewhat limited in their country. As part of the national system of wage controls applied shortly after the Second World War "a standardised method of job evaluation" was introduced, and a government board also found that "it had to lay down very detailed rules for ... incentives, merit grading, profit sharing ...".[3] This standard job evaluation system became well rooted and has tended to prevail in the country's labour relations. A few union officials did add, however, that in the Rotterdam area where a great expansion by multinational oil and chemical plants occurred in the 1960s, there was a tendency for some of these companies to bring with them important parts of their job evaluation and/or merit grading systems. The lack of a standard industry-wide collective agreement such as exists in metals may also help to account for this greater range of flexibility among petroleum and chemical companies.

While reactions to these special wage systems vary, many trade unionists indicated that they had some difficulty with them. They were less familiar with the criteria being employed, and in several cases they complained that the companies refused to make available the basis of the system, on the grounds that these were confidential. The unions felt themselves to be at more than arms length in their efforts to come to grip with such systems. The systems were not necessarily less favourable to employees; but some unions in Belgium, for example, complained about two European-based subsidiaries, one in electronics and one in food, which, they claimed, they were not able "to penetrate" for purposes of effective job-wage bargaining because of the more or less unique company wage systems.

At times, innovation by a multinational enterprise with a prevailing wage system can lead to labour difficulties. Mention has already been made that Ford and General Motors in the United Kingdom had innovated with their use of measured day work, while the great bulk of British automobile and engineering workers were on a payment by results system. When Chrysler took over the British Rootes company in 1967, "a strike broke out almost immediately in the Coventry works, due to a change from a piece rate system to the American practice of a measured day rate ..." according to one trade union report.[4] In actual fact, the changes sought by the Chrysler United Kingdom management went beyond the wage system; this was but one part of a larger effort to bring about in the United Kingdom, more company-wide, more standardised union-management relations and conditions, as against the more fragmented bargaining and conditions which existed in the Rootes plants.[5] As part of
----

[1] Gennard, in Flanagan and Weber, op. cit., p. 98, notes "... Two foreign-owned subsidiary innovations that spread quickly into the United Kingdom industrial relations system were productivity agreements and reform of pay structures on the basis of job evaluation ..." In both cases United States industrial engineering firms made a significant contribution.

[2] Turner (Graham), op. cit., p. 105. The companies in question are Shell, Unilever and Imperial Chemical Industries.

[3] W. Albeda, "Recent Trends in Collective Bargaining in the Netherlands", in ILO, Collective Bargaining ..., op. cit., pp. 320-321.

[4] Karl Casserini, "Multinational Companies and Collective Bargaining", in OECD, Trade Union Seminar on New Perspectives in Collective Bargaining, November 1969, Paris, Report No. 115, p. 4. Also see TUC ... International Companies ..., op. cit., p. 7, for a similar report on this strike at Chrysler.

[5] See for example the Financial Times, 24 May 1975, in which it was reported that union reservations about continuing company efforts to move toward "centrally co-ordinated negotiations in place of 53 separate ones" seemed to prolong a dispute over wages between Chrysler unions and management.

its programme to establish more company wide standards, Chrysler withdrew from the Engineering Employers' Federation not long after it took over Rootes.

Shearer reports about difficulties encountered by United States firms which "installed American systems of annual performance reviews for salary increases" in countries where customs "do not permit their operation as intended". He adds, that, for example, in countries like Italy, "it is unacceptable ... to pass over any individual for annual increases merely because of his unsatisfactory performance".[1]

The tendency to extend company systems and structures in wage and job administration appears to be particularly pronounced in the case of managerial and some white-collar employees in mutlinational subsidiaries. For managerial employees, but on occasion too, for white-collar employees (at least in the middle and upper salary ranges) some multinatinational enterprises apply a virtually uniform salary system around the world. This is confirmed by a number of unions and some employer representatives in most of the countries surveyed. A union of supervisory personnel in the United Kingdom complained that it finds some United States auto firms and a European based electronics company "immutable" in their grading systems for supervisors whom the union represents.

----

[1] Shearer, in Barkin et al, op. cit., p. 119.

CHAPTER V

THE MULTINATIONAL, A "SPECIAL PHENOMENON"
IN LABOUR RELATIONS?

It has so far been suggested that as a general rule, in most of the countries surveyed in this report, multinational enterprises conform or are compelled to conform, by a variety of forces, to most of the national labour practices in West European countries. At the same time it is also true that as regards many important individual labour practices, many multinationals do bring with them and put into practice in varying degrees some of their own (home country) policies, that on some matters they operate under home country control and direction, and that often their very styles of labour management show distinct home country traces and influence. It has also been indicated that as regards investment and production decisions, multinationals differ from national companies in some important respects.

Multinational companies are almost without exception organisations with substantial operations and long experience in their own countries. Part of their growth and success can be attributed to their handling of manpower and skills as well as technical processes. Professor Richard E. Caves, an eminent authority cn industrial organisation, in a conference on multinationals in the United Kingdom observed:

> ... The evidence then suggests, strongly, if in a general way, that superior labour relations (implemented in part through greater commitments of managerial talent) have been one source of the [multinationals'] subsidiaries' superior performance ... [Can] the subsidiaries' superior performance be tied specifically to their labour-management practices, or do these merely reflect a high level of managerial ability generally? Is the foreign firm adroit at labour relations because it brings the experience of operating in other national systems, or merely because it is efficient ...[1]

The multinational as innovator

The extent to which multinational company subsidiaries are innovators in the labour relations field is a matter of considerable debate between management and union officials. While multinational companies are generally looked upon as innovating institutions, employers argue that this innovation is found in technical, marketing and related fields, while the typical multinational pursues its labour policies in keeping with host country and local labour practice. On the other hand, some unions argue that multinationals will often bring with them parts, at least, of their home country labour practices.

While it is obvious that no multinational enterprise brings with it to Europe an entire panoply of labour relations practices and institutions, one does continually find pieces of evidence that such companies rarely shed all their home country practices. Moreover, in some labour areas the carry-over of home country practices is quite substantial.[2] Among some officials of multinational enterprises there are even jokes that as a result of the impact of company experience, company organisational structure, company training and other factors, you can recognise an "X company man" or a "Y company man" a mile away! There is doubtless some exaggeration here, but it helps make the point.

The style or philosophies which multinationals bring with them can be quite important in affording home offices some considerable degree of influence over host country personnel or industrial relations directors. In many cases it is clear that the labour officers of the host countries' subsidiaries (they are almost always local nationals in Western Europe) receive significant training within the multinational enterprise. Then, too, home office officials may have some voice in the selection of the host country top labour officials. Kenneth Walker, reporting

----

[1] Dunning (editor), op. cit., pp. 145-146.

[2] In this regard such general issues as union recognition, membership in host country employers' associations and specific collective bargaining issues such as wage and job administration, pensions, have already been discussed above.

on a meeting of management experts dealing with the multinational firm issue, writes that "the selection", the "assessment" and the "promotion of labour relations staff at the national [host country] level" is "one of the means" by which "some multinational companies exert an influence on the general labour policy and the approach of their" subsidiary companies, "while preserving the formal autonomy" of such subsidiaries.[1]

In a study of the overseas labour policies of major US automobile companies, Duane Kujawa reports that in the case of the Ford Motor Company the US Vice-President, labour relations staff, "approves the appointment of an individual as the labour relations director of Ford-England, the vice-president of labour relations at Ford-Canada, etc." These approvals are made on nominations by managing directors of the Ford subsidiaries in these various countries. The author notes this "approval is seldom if ever withheld".[2]

Visits between home and host country in both Ford and Chrysler according to Kujawa seem to be an important aspect of management development, including labour relations management. In the case of Chrysler's foreign industrial relations managers, he says:

Visits by foreign industrial relations managers to the United States home office represent a second type of management development activity. On these visits, the foreign executive spends time at both the corporate personnel office and the personnel departments in the plants. He observes first hand the manner in which the parent corporation handles its own labour affairs. Chrysler's personnel group tries to give the visitor as broad an exposure to its internal operations as time will allow. It stresses the method used in analysing different labour problems and in evaluating alternative solutions to them.[3]

The same author writes that for Ford, "a certain amount of training activity" consists of "visits to the foreign subsidiaries by US technical and managerial personnel to assist local managers in their labour relations administration ...". He cites, for example, Ford-Netherlands which "received some on-the-spot assistance from a Ford-US actuarial expert in 1967 when it was revising its retirement benefits programme". Or the case of the Canadian subsidiary which "reported a considerable amount of consultation with US technical and managerial personnel as various problems arose ...".[4]

The US overseas liaison manager of Ford makes visits abroad which are not classified as "training", and are more for the benefit of "updating" the US manager. But "since prior labour relations problems and their solutions are discussed at each of the subsidiaries he visits, there is quite naturally a management development dimension ...".[5] Labour relations managers from overseas "frequently visit the US headquarters of Ford, and these visits partake of a "general orientation" nature, or are "a problem-oriented visit".[6]

Summing up this process generally, one Ford international industrial relations executive commented that "the corporate staff share in the selection of key industrial relations personnel to assure their training and experience would prompt them to pursue broadly accepted principles of employee and trade union relations ...". He adds that new industrial relations management personnel spend time in a Ford plant (other than the one they work in) "to observe the application of approved principles and philosophies ...". The general result of these programmes is to

----

[1] OECD, _Labour Problems in Multinational Firms_, Report on a Meeting of Management Experts, Paris, 21 June 1973, p. 7.

[2] Kujawa, op. cit., pp. 97-99.

[3] Ibid., p. 39.

[4] Ibid., p. 101.

[5] Ibid.

[6] Ibid.

produce in Ford a "similar and predictable" but not a strictly "uniform" approach to labour problems in the company's subsidiaries abroad.[1]

Rotation of managerial personnel in multinationals

The practice referred to by the Ford official of broadening their management personnel's outlook by providing them with experience in another country is followed by some other multinationals which regularly rotate some of their managerial personnel from country to country.[2]

The International Organisation of Employers concludes from its questionnaire survey of multinational enterprises that several "make particular reference to their growing practice of moving their managerial staff not only between parent and subsidiary but from one subsidiary to another ... to give them international experience". It cites one example of a multinational enterprise which first seeks "to develop the nationals of each country to fill the majority of its managerial positions ..." thus pursuing a policy of "localisation". This is then followed by the "second step of 'internationalisation', i.e. that of mixing nationalities at the top of the subsidiary". The net "result of this policy is" that nearly half of its top management throughout the world have "had experience of working in a country other than their own - and these not by any means from the home country."[3]

Such shifting of managerial personnel can, at times, look like a different matter to workers and their unions. Unions in most of the countries visited in this survey complained about the greater rotation among managerial personnel of multinational enterprises, when compared to national companies. They felt this often disrupts their relations with management.

It does appear however that there may be less rotation among personnel and industrial relations managers than among some other groups. Almost all of the personnel management people are, to repeat, nationals of the host countries. But any substantial rotation of top management can have effects on the general structure of labour-management relations. In a report on the labour problems at one multinational company subsidiary, by a British government agency, it was noted, inter alia, that the factory:

... has experienced a number of changes among it top management, particularly among its works managers. In the past ten years, there have been seven works managers, the first of whom had held the post for the previous six years. While this movement has been unavoidable, the effect has been to produce uncertainty on the shop floor. Many shop stewards and employees commented on the problem of adapting to different styles of leadership, of reaching understandings with one works manager only to have them ignored by his successor ...

The report concludes: "It is almost a commonplace that instability among top management will produce uncertainty on the shop floor, as customary behaviour patterns are disturbed ...".[4]

While visits among management officials in the personnel and industrial relations sectors of multinationals have already been referred to above, periodical conferences of such personnel can also be a useful device to exchange experience and

----

[1] Paper presented by Robert Copp to Michigan State University Conference on Industrial Relations Problems of Multinational Corporations in Advanced Industrial Societies, November 1974.

[2] In her study of IBM, Nancy Foy writes that within the company it is sometimes stated that "IBM stands for I've been moved"! See The IBM World (London, Eyre, Methuen, Ltd., 1974), p. 139.

[3] IOE, op. cit., pp. 14-15. Also see p. 21 of ibid. for further references of the opportunities provided for managerial staff of multinationals to work outside their own countries.

[4] Commission on Industrial Relations, Report No. 11, Hoover Limited, November 1970 (London, HMSO, 1970), pp. 7-8.

ensure some degree of consistency in approach. In the present survey of Western Europe there were numerous reports that it was fairly common for multinationals to convene such periodical European-wide conferences of their personnel or industrial relations managers.

Policy manuals, guides and other forms of written instruction can be another device or method to ensure central guidance and/or understanding of basic company principles among subsidiaries. Such guides or manuals (sometimes called pre-policy manuals) were noted as being utilised in several multinational enterprises touched upon by the present survey.[1]

One area in which multinationals generally lead most other companies is in the amount and range of training of personnel they undertake. It appears to be more common among some multinationals, too, to provide a large share or at least important parts of this training on an in-house basis. Many make less use of host country training facilities than is true of national firms; this may be a characteristic of nearly all large firms as opposed to smaller firms but many multinational plants are part of larger firms. This emphasis on training may be part of the multinational's need to assure articulation of its many geographically separated units. A few important multinational enterprises have established their own international training centres.

Multinationals, styles and philosophies

By these and related devices, consciously or unconsciously, it is clear that many multinationals extend their styles and philosophies of labour relations to a considerable degree even where no attempt is made directly to influence day-to-day decisions of subsidiaries. It would appear that without some such central philosophy or general guidance, many would operate with greater difficulty. The top international industrial relations executive of a Canadian-based engineering firm has explained that "without basic corporate policy - a 'grand design' for the enterprise as a whole - and consistent functional policy subsidiary to it, a truly integrated world-wide enterprise cannot be built". He adds: "there are particularly compelling reasons for common industrial relations policies at all locations in the international enterprise". The "shrinkage of time and space" and the great development of "modern communication" make it "important that the company should take a consistent position on principle in its relations with individual employees and employee representatives at all locations". Such consistency "avoids, for example, the company taking a strike in Coventry on an issue of principle conceded to the union in Detroit". He cited the case of a "well-known North American-based international company which accepted a strike rather than concede" that "union membership was a condition of employment ... in its British plant". At the same time this same company had already conceded a "full union shop" in their Canadian plant, "a Taft-Hartley union shop" in the United States and a "full closed shop in Australia".[2]

On the point of consistency, Kujawa writes of Ford that "one of its unwritten policies regarding collective labour negotiations at foreign subsidiaries" is "that subsidiary management will conduct labour relations negotiations in such a manner that positions it takes on certain issues are not prejudicial to Ford management in other parts of the world ....[3]

The international personnel director of Philips, the Dutch-based multi-national, has also written about the aim of a "certain consensus" on "personnel and industrial relations" matters which his company strives for:
----

[1] A management personnel specialist reporting to a conference on multinationals at the International Institute of Labour Studies stated: "For personnel and industrial relations to have effective direction and consistency, to be a fully integrated part of general management, they must work to a clear common policy which should be: (1) applicable throughout the enterprise in all countries; (2) in writing ...". See Hans Günter, editor, Transnational Industrial Relations (London, MacMillan, 1972), p. 101. There appears to be considerable variation between multinationals so far as the use of formal written manuals or guides to labour policy are concerned.

[2] Jack Belford, Vice-President, Personnel and Industrial Relations, Massey-Ferguson Ltd., Address to a Loyola University Conference, July 1968, pp. 6-7.

[3] Kujawa, op. cit., p. 112.

- 39 -

... [Although] ... social policies primarily take shape on an individual national basis, there is a concern personnel industrial relations service which aims at a certain consensus about the underlying basic considerations, acts as a clearing-house of knowledge and experience and provides advice and assistance.[1]

As one example of how such company industrial relations policy or philosophy might operate, the aforementioned executive of the Canadian engineering company indicated that his organisation was generally opposed to the use of binding arbitration procedures to resolve disputes over interest questions (the negotiation of new contract terms and so forth). Confronted some years ago with the long-established Australian compulsory arbitration system of interest disputes and in keeping with the company's home policy, its Australian management was, however, able "in fact to contract out of the arbitration act" by negotiating an agreement which limited arbitration to disputes over issues of rights only. This fits in with the company's philosophy. Obviously the union involved had agreed to this, but the unusual departure from the Australian labour pattern clearly had its impulse in the "principles" which derive from the company's North American experience.[2]

The manner in which home office labour philosophies and experiences can differ with national practices in host countries is illustrated in the definition which one company executive proposed as to the scope of "industrial relations questions" for a recent conference on multinational company labour relations problems. These were, he stated, questions which -

... concern remuneration and conditions of employment, including employee benefit plans; recruitment and training of employees; recognition of trade union or other employee representatives; establishment of collective bargaining and grievance resolution procedures; and resolution of disputes that might arise concerning these matters.[3]

He went on to say explicitly, "management decisions about new or redeployed production facilities are not, as such, industrial relations questions". He did add "the effects of these decisions on employees" could be the subject of bargaining.

As it happens in several European countries included in the present survey, management decisions about "new or redeployed production facilities" now fall within the scope of industrial relations institutions and questions, and they involve union inputs into these decisions (reference is made here for example to different forms of worker participation on company supervisory boards in the Federal Republic of Germany or Sweden). What appears to be a definition of industrial relations growing out of experience in North America may not be adequate in some other contexts.

If North American multinational companies seem to stand out more than others, it is due, in part, to their somewhat more unique labour experiences (when compared, for example, with multinationals home-based in continental Western Europe) and consequent managerial styles. A recent survey by _Fortune_ suggests that multinationals from a country like Japan, which also has a rather unique labour system and management style, are also more likely to bring such a style and some labour practices with them.[4]

----

[1] P.L. Dronkers, "A Multinational Organisation and Industrial Relations: The Philips Case", paper prepared for the International Industrial Relations Association, Third World Congress, London, 2-3 September 1973, p. 1.

[2] Belford (Loyola Conference), op. cit., pp. 12-14.

[3] Paper presented by Robert Copp to Michigan State University Conference on Industrial Relations Problems of Multinational Corporations in Advanced Industrial Societies, November 1974.

[4] "The Japanese are coming with their own style of management", _Fortune Magazine_, March 1975, p. 116 et seq. _Fortune_ was referring here to Japanese MNEs operating in the US market.

The_multinational,_a_special_challenge
to_the_union

When compared with average companies in Western Europe, multinationals tend to have more complex industrial relations functions, larger and more often "internally" oriented training systems, career ladders, special company benefit and wage plans and often more detailed communication systems. The net effect of these factors is to create, in at least some countries, a sense that the multinationals are more "integrated" establishments.

Trade unionists in three countries specifically use this term "integrated", independently of each other, in describing some of their difficulties in dealing with multinational enterprises. A similar phenomenon was also referred to in two of the other three countries surveyed.

Clearly one could hardly object, as such, to companies which have more extensive training programmes, or to companies which have their own special benefit programmes.[1] From a union point of view what tends to be created by a combination of these and other factors sometimes seems to be a company fortress able to stand in a high degree of isolation from the union's thrust to share in the administration of labour practices in the company.

Because of these factors, unions find it more difficult to "penetrate" such companies. Even where the union is recognised, at a number of multinational enterprises in Belgium, the Netherlands and, to some extent, the United Kingdom, there are complaints that workers' representatives have a more difficult time in "penetrating" the company in terms of union or worker influence.

The_multinational,_a_"special_world"?

The multinational enterprise has in effect some of the characteristics of a "special world" of its own. In writing about "multinational subculture", P.J. Gordon suggests that when studying these enterprises "doubt can arise ... whether one is simply looking at an Italian firm, for example in looking at Olivetti ..." or "whether one is simply looking at another large company, the characteristics of which might be influenced by technology and the very international environments of the operation ...". Professor Pieter Hessling adds: "From multinational headquarters certain values, attitudes and assumptions seem to be disseminated which form a layer upon the national culture and create a new identity for the bearers".[2]

At least as regards labour relations behaviour in Western Europe this characterisation may go a bit too far, but it helps explain the reactions of national unions to many multinational subsidiary plants.

Some studies of specific companies support Hessling's general characterisation of multinational enterprises subculture. A recent book on the International Business Machine Company, for example, in explaining the special quality and success of that firm, notes:

The book is really about IBM culture. My own conclusion is that external forces such as anti-trust suits in the United States or economic nationalism abroad weigh less in IBM's ultimate success than the attention it pays to internal forces, built into this culture ...[3]

----

[1] In the Netherlands, all three unions visited (the factory workers' unions of all three Dutch confederations) specifically expressed the opinion that the special benefits and generally high wage rates established by several multinationals which did not recognise unions were part of those companies' campaigns to keep the unions out. This same view was voiced in the United Kingdom by several unions which had been unsuccessful in obtaining recognition at a few multinational enterprises.

[2] Pieter Hessling (Professor of Organisational Behaviour, Rotterdam University), Organisational_Behaviour_and_Culture,_the_Case_of_Multinational_Enterprise, lecture delivered on 28 January 1971, p. 12. The quotation of Gordon is from Hessling's paper.

[3] Foy, op. cit., p. XV.

The author adds:

... the travelling IBMer can walk into the IBM office in Bangkok or Beirut and find someone who speaks his language ... The office will look the same and people inside will talk his language, not only English but IBMese ... The corporate culture runs beneath the national culture, seldom visible from outside unless one knows its characteristics ...[1]

Even if one concedes that IBM may be an extreme case of a special company culture, many other multinational companies are like it in some respects.

To carry this special corporate process to the labour relations level, the policy of high benefits, special training programmes, special company parties, internal house organs and the like create a special kind of attachment of workers to such enterprises. In turn this may lead to disinterest on the part of workers in the ordinary union organisations of the country. A Belgian survey of multinational subsidiaries in that country concludes that these conditions in multinationals create what it calls "the policy of integration of these [foreign] enterprises at the level of human relations". The relatively good "conditions offered to workers by the foreign employer make inoperative a good number of material demands which constitute one of the most important elements of working class unity". This "policy of attachment to the foreign enterprise can encourage a certain disaffection of workers towards their organisations". Relatedly, it favours individual rather than collective attachments and this too of course weakens the appeal of unionism.[2]

The multinational, an integrated force?

As has been suggested elsewhere in this report, with regard to other aspects of the multinational enterprise, it is also true that especially in some smaller countries the unions express themselves most strongly about these unique "integrating" characteristics. It is probably in part the relatively large role such companies play in Belgium and to some extent in Dutch economic life that helps account for the reactions to these companies. In the Belgian metal fabricating industry for example, the leading metal employers' association estimates that multinationals account for around 50 per cent of employment, nearly two-thirds of shipments and approximately two-thirds of the industry's exports. US-based multinationals alone account for about one-fourth of the same industry's employment, sales and exports.[3]

While multinational enterprises are not so great a force in the British or Swedish economies, the problem of their special "integrated" character was raised by some unionists. In France the Confédération Générale du Travail similarly complains:

The multinationals are playing an important role in the formulation, transmission and experimentation of methods directed at integrating the workers and their unions. In this respect, the American multinationals have played a not negligible role in introducing into Europe new methods of human relations, and often play a leading part in employing these methods, as in the case of the concept known as 'management by objectives'.[4]

----

[1] Ibid., pp. 6-7. See the remainder of this book for illustrations of how this corporate culture pervades IBM's subsidiaries everywhere.

[2] Beckers et al, op. cit., pp. 64-65. Unionists from both the socialist and catholic metal unions in Belgium, independently of each other, used the phrase "patriotisme de l'entreprise" to characterise the shielded nature of many such companies.

[3] Fabrimetal, September 1974, p. 20. The Federation of Swedish Industries survey shows that "foreign-owned companies accounted for 33 per cent of total industrial turnover" in Belgium, 18.9 per cent in Holland and only 9.7 per cent and 9.1 per cent in Sweden and Great Britain respectively. The Multinationals in Sweden (Stockholm, 1973), p. 13. (The dates of the data varied slightly for each country, but this is not likely to influence the general relationships.)

[4] CGT, op. cit. (pages not numbered).

To the argument that what has been described as the special characteristics of multinationals may all be mere characteristics of large companies, multi-plant and not just multinational, there are at least several counter points. In the first place, as this report has elsewhere noted, multinational subsidiaries are generally part of larger companies. Secondly, large companies that grow up at home are in their home operations inherently part of the national industrial relations culture as are the unions that deal with them. Moreover, unions do not make the same charges against large nationally based companies that they do against multinationals. Finally, there is not the same feeling on the part of unions in dealing with a national company that important decisions are made from a distance, at a central headquarters outside the country.

Conversations with local union leaders sometimes point at this somewhat special quality of "distance". A German leader of a works council at a US home-based auto plant subsidiary reported that the US company readily accepted the works council and the regional metal-working collective agreement in the Federal Republic of Germany; but every now and again in negotiations about some problem, he asserted, would come the remark, "but the company just doesn't do it that way in Detroit!" A local trade unionist at another subsidiary in the United Kingdom declared that for years the local management insisted there was no dependence on its home country office and all operations at the subsidiary had to stand on their own. Yet at a critical moment when an expansaion programme was under contemplation and local funds were lacking, a large injection of investment funds from the home office was suddenly forthcoming. Remarks or comments similar to these, reinforcing the uneasy sense that critical decision-making power lay outside the country, were often made by other local plant unionists at multinational subsidiaries. Many incidents were cited wherein negotiations were interrupted so that, according to union negotiators, host country management could consult their home offices before making final commitments on one issue or another.

It is the somewhat special "world unto itself" character of multinational enterprises that helps account for the sharp reactions of many union leaders to them, especially on the public level, nearly everywhere in Western Europe. Of course, there are differences between multinationals which may relate to industrial-technological factors, their country of origin, their "age" in a particular location and so forth and these factors modify what has just been described; but what has been described in this section is a basic, general characteristic of numbers of multinational enterprises which may influence their labour relations in many subtle ways.

CHAPTER VI

UNION AND EMPLOYER EXPERIENCES AND
ATTITUDES ON TRANSNATIONAL LABOUR RELATIONS

In surveying union and company attitudes on such issues as the desirability or possibility of developing transnational labour relations at multinational enterprises, any research effort faces some handicaps. Kenneth Walker, reporting on an OECD management seminar on the "Labour Problems in Multinational Firms" observed that on a matter like this (the development of transnational labour relations), "The initiative is with the unions ...". The unions, he writes, "have an agenda and a goal ...". On the other hand, the companies have no such agenda or goals, since they generally are not favourable to this possible development.[1]

Under these circumstances, it is therefore not surprising that it is easier to find union reports and resolutions on this subject than it is to find comparable management positions. As a result, a chapter such as this one may tend to be weighted somewhat more heavily with union statements of position and attitude.

*   *   *

It is difficult to summarise briefly the attitudes of union leaders towards the broad, general labour relations issues concerning multinational enterprises. The position of the ordinary union leader contrasts with that of the multinational company officer. The latter functions in an organisation whose very structure and operations compel him to think in transnational terms a very large part of the time. As opposed to this the union leader's basic power as well as his day to day, even most of his year to year, experience is centred in a national environment. Even when the union leader is questioned about multinational labour problems it may involve a special "leap" of the mind for him to address such problems in truly multinational terms.

The national union leader is much more likely to adapt to or partake of extra-national or multinational labour processes during those relatively infrequent occasions when he becomes part of an international labour meeting, as for example in a congress of an international trade union secretariat (ITS), a transnational union meeting covering representatives from a particular multinational company, a world labour confederation congress or an ILO meeting.

This survey does not, for example, describe in any detail the positions which the national union leaders and their organisations have taken on transnational bargaining in meetings of various ITSs, positions which occasionally support some such bargaining. But it is important to bear this aspect of the unionists' positions in mind.[2]

The great bulk of the union officers surveyed in this report saw little hope or prospect for full-scale or very substantial transnational collective bargaining with multinational companies, at least for the time being. The relatively good wages and benefits at most multinational enterprises, moreover, left most of the unions surveyed feeling that there was no pressing need for anything like full-scale transnational bargaining. On the other hand, practically all of the unions surveyed have been involved in a series of activities which partake of pieces of transnational bargaining or consultation either with companies or with unions from other countries, and most of them look to the further development of certain aspects of transnational relationships between labour and multinational enterprises.

----

[1] OECD, Labour Problems in Multinational Firms, Report on a Meeting of Management Experts, Paris, 21-23 June 1972, p. 9.

[2] See for example the resolutions on multinational companies, especially those parts dealing with possible meetings and bargaining with such companies in: International Metalworkers' Federation, Minutes, 22nd International Congress, Lausanne, 26-30 October 1971, pp. 141-145, and IMF, Resolutions adopted at the 23rd Congress, Stockholm, 1974, pp. 21-26.

A number of union leaders in Belgium and the Netherlands are exceptions to the generalisation about the prospects or at least the need for wider and more rapid development of transnational bargaining. These Dutch and Belgian unionists felt more "threatened" by multinational power, and seem to favour a much more rapid development of multinational labour relations with such enterprises.

In explaining this greater willingness of Dutch and Belgian trade union leaders to favour a wider transnationalisation of labour relations with multi-national enterprises, one must refer again to the much greater role such companies play in the economies of these two countries as compared to most others in Western Europe.

Moreover, in addition to the greater density of multinationals, the relatively smaller size of these countries may make them more dependent upon multinational plants in other countries so far as labour matters are concerned. In very recent years Dutch workers at the Ford Motor Company, Amsterdam plant, have found that a strike or any slow-down in the British Ford Motor Company's division can lead to a similar slow-down or shut-down of Ford operations in the Netherlands, within a week in some cases. Even the British coal strike which led to reduced manufacturing operations in that country quickly resulted in a substantial shut-down of Ford's Amsterdam operations according to Dutch trade unionists. Somewhat similar is the relationship and dependence of the even larger Ford Genk plant in Belgium upon its "mother" company, namely the Ford Motor Company of the Federal Republic of Germany with headquarters in Cologne. It is not suggested that all multinational plants in Belgium and the Netherlands are so tightly integrated with those in larger European countries or the United States, but even if a high degree of integration is true in only a handful of cases, this can shape basic union attitudes.

In the minds of most unions surveyed there were a number of barriers to anything like full-scale transnational collective bargaining with multinational enterprises. These include: the relatively good wages and working conditions in most multinational subsidiaries (in the food and metal-working industries covered in this survey); the existence of plural unionism and plural international union affiliations in most of Western Europe; the nature of bargaining structures in their own countries; legal obstacles to transnational union action; the great costs of bringing trade unionists together even for preliminary meetings to plan strategy and tactics; language barriers - these were among the most serious of such obstacles.

Inter-union structural obstacles to
transnational bargaining

The existence of "plural" unionism in a substantial number of West European countries may represent an obstacle to the potential development of transnational union-management relations. In Belgium, France, the Netherlands and Italy, and in some other West European countries, unions are divided along ideological and/or religious lines, and it is common for several unions to represent workers in the same occupational classifications at a given firm. Such divisions can make transnational approaches to management difficult. It is not only that these unions may at times be in conflict over strategy and tactics in their national activities; often these same unions have different international affiliations (some belong to the International Trade Union Secretariats - ITSs - which are loosely affiliated to the International Confederation of Free Trade Unions - ICFTU - some to the Trade Unions Internationals - TUIs - of the World Federation of Trade Unions - WFTU - and some to the comparable bodies of the World Confederation of Labour - WCL), and this makes co-operation at the international level more difficult. On the other hand recent developments such as the formation of the European Trade Union Confederation and the enlargement of the European Metalworkers' Federation (EMF) which embrace unions of different ideological and religious persuasions indicate that some of these barriers are perhaps being overcome, to some extent, at the European level. Indeed the EMF has already been a participant in several meetings with multinational enterprises.[1]

The nature of national union structures in a single country may also retard the development of the kind of solidarity vis-à-vis multinationals which would seem to be a requisite for making substantial transnational bargaining approaches. Thus,

[1] Some of these meetings are described in the next chapter.

in the United Kingdom where craft unionism tends to be so predominant in many industries, it may be more difficult to build transnational union solidarity vis-à-vis certain multinational enterprises. Within many multinational metal-working companies in the United Kingdom, for example, no single union has a sufficient standing to act as a very effective rallying point for transnational action in relation to such companies.[1]

Bargaining structures and strategies as obstacles to transnationalism

One can find several examples of national union bargaining structures or strategies which, to a degree at least, represent obstacles to the development of transnational bargaining approaches. As a first case one may take the metalworkers' union in the Federal Republic of Germany and the transnational automobile companies. This union has been a participant in all of the important work of the International Metalworkers' Federation in the multinational field; the German union has participated in the formation of the IMF auto company world councils, the regional auto meetings and IMF individual company council meetings. Yet the fact remains that this union's basic bargaining is done within the Federal Republic of Germany on a broad regional basis with relevant employers' associations. The union is hardly in a position to lift out subsidiary plants of a multinational auto company and line these up for transnational company-type bargaining on a wide range of issues. It is not of course suggested here that either this union of the Federal Republic of Germany or its associated unions in the IMF have proposed such full-scale transnational negotiations with automobile companies. The example is cited merely to show some potential difficulties.[2]

There have been on the other hand increasing tendencies among workers and their organisations in large German auto plants and in many other large plants in Western Europe to take greater initiatives to influence both wages and working conditions at the plant level, over and beyond what is provided by regional or national agreements. This tendency towards a growing degree of plant and company bargaining "separatism" improves the opportunity for at least some transnational co-operation in Western Europe, between unionists at plants of the same company in different countries.[3]

Writing on this development of greater enterprise bargaining in the United Kingdom, B.C. Roberts states, "it is the almost simultaneous development of establishment and enterprise bargaining in Britain and Europe and the vast growth of

----

[1] The existence of a general, combined section of British metal-working unions in the IMF overcomes this problem to a limited extent.

[2] The German Federation of Trade Unions (DGB) has recently stated its views on the manner in which national bargaining structures limit any possibilities of broad supranational bargaining: "International co-ordination of trade union policy vis-à-vis multinational firms finds its limitation when it comes to the question of standardising the duration of collective agreements, and possibly the standardisation of collective agreements themselves. Such attempts would presuppose the standardisation of collective bargaining procedures and of the way in which they are organised, and would also leave out of account both the importance of the traditional forms of the labour struggle, which can vary considerably from one country to another, and also the forms of labour legislation governing labour disputes in the various countries. Such attempts would be tantamount to undermining the strike power of the national trade unions, without providing any substitute to act in compensation at the international level ...". "Resolutions of the Tenth Regular Congress of the DGB", Hamburg, 25-31 May 1975, in ICFTU Economic and Social Bulletin, Vol. XXIII, No. 3, May-June 1975, pp. 3-4.

[3] On the increasing importance of enterprise-level bargaining see: ILO, Collective Bargaining ..., op. cit., p. 89; E.M. Kassalow, "Conflict and Co-operation in Europe's Industrial Relations", Industrial Relations (Berkeley), Vol. 13, No. 2, May 1974; Norman F. Dufty, Changes in Labour-Management Relations in the Enterprise (Paris, OECD, 1975).

the multinational corporations which has made the extension of collective bargaining across national frontiers possible."[1]

As far as obstacles in bargaining structure are concerned, one can also mention some union-management institutions and policies in Sweden. In that country, for example, the Metalworkers' Union is part of the general bargaining framework for economic benefits which covers nearly all privately employed industrial workers who are represented by the Swedish Confederation of Trade Unions (LO). The latter reaches one general bargain with the Swedish Employers' Association (SAF). Within that framework the metalworkers' union and the LO have supported the solidarity wage principle. The latter is oriented to the concept that workers should be paid the same wage for comparable work under similar conditions, regardless of the industry in which they are employed. In other words, a skilled mechanic should receive more or less the same wage regardless of the manufacturing industry or company in which he is employed. The same would hold for semi-skilled or unskilled workers[2], i.e. within their own skill ranges they should receive approximately equal wages regardless of industry or company.

It would be difficult to reconcile such a general principle of wage policy with efforts to negotiate wages on a transnational basis for a particular multinational company.[3] Again it is not suggested that the Swedish metal union in its work with IMF has called for transnational wage bargaining. The case is cited only to show some of the potential obstacles.

To take an example where differences in strategy might be an obstacle to transnational labour evolution one can cite a discussion which took place in the 1973 meeting of the IMF Chrysler World Auto Council. One group of delegates at this meeting proposed that the council adopt the goal of working for a common expiration date for all collective agreements covering Chrysler plants regardless of country. Such a tactic it was contended would improve the unions' bargaining strength vis-à-vis this company. Several British delegates at this meeting opposed this suggestion and argued that common expiration dates could "put tremendous financial pressure" on the unions, if a strike occurred at the point of a common expiration date.[4]

In conversations during the course of this ILO survey some other British trade unionists expressed preference, just as a tactical matter, for expiration dates at different times at different plants of the same company, to allow unions constantly to improve their settlements over those previously achieved. However, by no means are all British unionists opposed to this principle of seeking common expiration dates, and this case is merely cited to illustrate a type of strategic barrier to transnational bargaining which can exist among some unions.

Union positions on transnational meetings with companies

While some of the policies of the German and Swedish metalworkers' unions have been cited to illustrate potential obstacles to some aspects of transnational union-management relations, both these organisations continue to support the numerous programmes of the International Metalworkers' Federation to strengthen co-operation among its affiliates in their relations with multinational enterprises. The Swedish union has also formulated its own programme to cope with multinationals. It has called, for example, for the establishment of "concern committees" to be set up at multinational enterprises, and it insists that "multinational companies should meet
----

[1] B.C. Roberts, "Multinational Collective Bargaining: A European Prospect", British Journal of Industrial Relations, Vol. XI, No. 1, March 1973, pp. 18-19.

[2] See Rudolf Meidner and Berndt Ohman, Swedish Trade Union Confederation LO, 15 Years of Wage Policy (Stockholm, 1972).

[3] On this problem of reconciling national and transnational objectives see the interesting exchange between Hans-Göran Myrdal of the Swedish Employers' Confederation (SAF) and Jan Olsson of the Swedish Metalworkers' Union, in The Multinational and the Swedish Labour Market (Stockholm, 1973).

[4] IMF, Meeting of the Chrysler World Auto Council, 10-11 May 1973, Geneva, pp. 8-11. Several unions supported the proposal for common expiration dates but no agreement was reached and the issue was deferred.

the cost of international co-operation between employees involving their own firms ...".[1]

A call similar to that of the Swedish union for regular transnational meetings between top multinational company management and union representatives has also been voiced by a number of other organisations. The World Confederation of Labour (WCL) has included in its proposed code to regulate multinationals a provision which would impose on these companies the "obligation of holding a yearly meeting (at the company's cost) of all the trade union delegates of the group". The European Trade Union Confederation (ETUC) has advocated legislation that "should ensure that, at the request of the trade union in the enterprise of the concern" and of "their international organisation", there should be created a body for the information and consultation of employees ...".[2]

The position of the World Federation of Trade Unions and its various affiliated bodies on the question of such transnational meetings between unions and management of multinational enterprises seems less clear. At a recent congress of the WFTU's Trade Unions International of Workers in the Metal Industry a preparatory document was available for the congress's consideration as regards multinational companies; it included union rights of "forcing the multinational company ... [to] have regular meetings organised between the management of the multinational company and the representatives of national and international trade union organisations", in order "to study all the questions that might have repercussions on the workers' positions (investments, evolution of the production, etc. ...)." The final resolutions and declaration of this conference while including a number of proposals to strengthen international trade union solidarity to combat multinational companies made no reference to this proposal for such regular meetings with multinational enterprises.[3] This TUI has also called for the development of a "charter of trade union rights in the face of multinational companies". The WFTU itself in 1973 adopted a general "charter of trade union rights" and it includes a section on multinationals; but this section does not make any reference to or call for meetings between unions and multinationals.[4]

In his testimony before the United Nations Eminent Persons Inquiry into Multinationals, the WFTU representative favoured "the right to international bargaining for workers in enterprises belonging to economic groups operating in different countries or at the level of regional economic groupings", but he dismissed the UN Report's "ambiguous formulation regarding the so-called 'multinational trade unions' ...". He declared that "on the contrary" to deal with multinationals "there was a need to strengthen trade union action at the country level ..." and this would assist "co-ordinated action at the international level". Asked whether he thought "Unions should share in the management of enterprises" he expressed his opposition, stating this would be but "dust in the eyes of workers" and make them responsible for decisions "imposed by the owners of enterprises in the light of their exclusive preoccupation with profits". Workers could "exercise an influence on management only through independent union action and pressure". Unions
----

[1] Swedish Metalworkers' Union, op. cit., p. 19.

[2] WCL, For a policy to cope with multinational companies (Brussels, 1973), p. 10; ETUC, "Workers' right of participation of multinational companies", resolution adopted by ETUC Executive Committee, 6 February 1975 (text is in ICFTU, Economic and Social Bulletin, Vol. XXIII, January-March 1975, p. 15).

[3] The Trade Unions International of Workers in the Metal Industries, Seventh International Conference; second item of the agenda: "For an efficient action by metalworkers and their trade unions against multinational corporations"; and on the actual programme and resolutions adopted see Metalworking unions in Action, Bulletin No. 1 and No. 2, 1975.

[4] WFTU, Eighth World Trade Union Congress, Bulgaria, 15-22 October 1973, Drafts of the Documents submitted for Discussion including II, Charter of Trade Union Rights, especially pp. 22-23, on multinationals. At a January 1975 meeting of the WFTU Executive Bureau, the organisation did propose "new trade union rights" vis-à-vis multinationals, including: "... the right to negotiate with the managements of multinational companies on any problems which concern the workers of the whole group". See: WFTU, The worsening of the crisis in the capitalist world, Document of the extraordinary session of the WFTU Bureau, Berlin, GDR, 28-29 January 1975 (Prague, 1975), p. 13.

had the right "to be informed" of enterprise decisions and in particular "to be told in advance of any decisions by the firm in respect of jobs, working conditions and the interests of the workers in general ...". But he opposed any "ambiguous structures" which seek to "integrate unions into the managing bodies of enterprises ...".[1]

This position on workers' participation in management contrasts with that taken by most of the affiliates of the ICFTU in Western Europe. Unions in the Federal Republic of Germany, Sweden and Norway, for example, already participate on supervisory boards of many companies in their own countries. Most of the ICFTU unions have also pressed the European Economic Community to extend such participation to multinational companies operating in more than one European country. Several unions see this as one device to obtain some voice in and greater information about multinational enterprises.

Transnational union meetings directed
at multinational enterprises

One of the significant union "responses" to the growth of multinational subsidiaries abroad has been to promote international "company-type" meetings of their own. To such meetings which deal with different plants of a given multinational enterprise in different countries, unions from different countries send representatives. Most such meetings have been convened by the international trade union secretariats, but on occasion, shop stewards in different European countries have acted on their own to call such inter-country union meetings. The general objective of these meetings is to exchange information and, in some cases, to co-ordinate union strategy vis-à-vis a particular multinational enterprise.[2]

On a few occasions the unions have encountered some difficulties with companies in obtaining permission for their representatives who work in the plants to attend such transnational union meetings. In a recent IMF meeting of its own SKF group of unions (held in the Federal Republic of Germany, 9-11 September 1975), the unions have charged that the management of that company's subsidiary in France denied trade union representatives permission to attend the meeting in Germany.[3]

Union demands for greater information from
multinationals

A virtually universal concern expressed by unions covered in this survey was the lack of sufficient information available on multinational companies. Many would echo the words of a top-level Dutch Catholic union officer who when opening a conference on unions and multinationals stated: "The weakness of our position is due in particular to our defective knowledge of the structure of these corporations, ... their decision-making centres and decision-making procedures ...". Unions, he added, lacked an "understanding of the different groups and pressures that set the tone for corporate management ...". He also complained that unions lack "insight" into the "criteria that prevail in management and long-term planning ..." within multinational enterprises.[4]

----

[1] Statement and questions and answers of Albertino Masetti, in United Nations, Summary of the hearings before the group of eminent persons to study the impact of multinational corporations on development and on international relations, ST/ESA/15 (New York), United Nations, 1974, pp. 316 and 322.

[2] A description of some of the multinational automobile company council meetings convened by the International Metalworkers' Federation is to be found in Kassalow, The International Metalworkers' Federation and the multinational auto companies, op. cit., passim.

[3] IMF, News, No. 16, September 1975. The IMF charges that the French delegates "were prevented from attending by SKF management in France ... even if they took unpaid leave".

[4] W.J.L. Spit in Tudyka, editor, op. cit., p. XI. For a discussion of union needs and fears vis-à-vis MNE investment, production and related employment decisions, see above, Chapter IV.

The French CGT also complains about the difficulty of obtaining information on the financial status of multinational companies:

> The complexity governing transfers of funds between companies of the same multinational group and their manipulation of taxes mean that it is particularly difficult for the representatives of the workers to acquire information on the economic activities of these companies. Their practices mean that the information furnished to works committees, for example, are devoid of all useful content.[1]

Some German trade unionists at the local level who worked for multinational subsidiaries where workers were represented on the supervisory boards of their particular plants were a little less concerned about information flows from multinationals; but even in the Federal Republic of Germany trade unionists generally were of the opinion that they were not well informed about over-all parent company structures, policy and practices.

Only recently, the German Federation of Trade Unions (DGB), for example, put great emphasis upon information as being "indispensable" for establishing the necessary controls over multinational companies. To this end, the DGB "supports international agreements ... making it compulsory for large companies ... to comply with certain requirements and standards in the matter of information, advertising, consultation and other forms of conduct ... vis-à-vis the public and the trade union ...". It believes "voluntary arrangements by multinational companies" to accomplish this end "are to be welcomed", but they are not "a lasting or final solution ...". It calls for international and national regulations and legislation to achieve these ends. The DGB also contends that "the trade unions concerned" with multinationals "must have rights of information, consultation, control and co-determination ... institutionalised on an international scale", in relation to "the operations of the parent companies of multinationals ...". Until such international measures exist, the DGB will seek such rights in "a national context".[2]

The ICFTU and its trade union secretariats have argued that any "multi-laterally negotiated charter laying down guidelines and rules of conduct" for multinationals should include the "obligation to publish global, accurate and comparable financial accounts and statistics of wage rates and social conditions obtaining in each of their branches".[3]

Complaints about lack of sufficient information are frequently made by those unions which deal with large multinational food manufacturing companies. Such complaints were articulated, for example, by a number of European trade union leaders during one of the earliest discussions of the multinational issues which took place within the International Union of Food and Allied Workers' Associations.[4]

The International Metalworkers' Federation working in co-operation with the Dutch Trade Union Confederation, NVV, and the latter's affiliated Industriebond and the German metalworkers' union (IG Metall) has prepared a manual setting forth what information unions demand of multinational enterprises.[5]

Among the principal data required from multinationals, this jointly produced manual lists:

> ... separate reports on both the multinational enterprise itself and its subsidiaries; listing of principal shareholders as well as participation of the multinational in other companies through "financial, marketing or technical links ..."; listing of all plants including types of production and

---

[1] CGT, op. cit. (no page numbers).

[2] "Resolution of Tenth Regular Congress of the DGB", 1975, op. cit., p. 2.

[3] "ICFTU/ITS Statement on Multinational Companies", in ICFTU, Economic and Social Bulletin, Vol. XXII, No. 1, January-February 1974, p. 25-26.

[4] See the discussion in the IUFD, Fourteenth Statutory Congress, Stockholm, 27-30 May 1964 (Geneva, Secretariat, 1964), pp. 98-121.

[5] IMF, Information to be covered by the System of Public Accountability on Multinational Companies (Geneva, 1975).

"employment figures" for all establishments, with individual establishments' employment to be "broken down into manual and non-manual", sex, skill, semi-skill, unskilled, indigenous and non-indigenous as well as "number of nationals from the parent company"; financial data on "capital foundation, profitability ... as well as indications for capital movements within the group structure"; data "to clearly reveal the company's solvency and liquidity" as well as careful profit and loss statements both on a "consolidated" and "individual company" basis; data on cash flow as well as debts, net worth, dividend payments; ...[1]

The manual continues by specifying general standards for how the balance sheet and profit and loss statement should be prepared. Financial reports should also include a section on future plans including forecasts for "increases or decreases in production [and] product development ..." with the possible effects "on employment" to "be quantified".[2]

For each company of the multinational enterprise the manual would require information to be made available on "Labour-management relations with special regard to trade union recognition, remuneration systems [and] working conditions." The latter to include inter alia work time, overtime rates, safety and health standards as well as accident rates, hiring and lay-off policy.[3]

Much of the unions' support for the work of the ITSs, their participation in transnational company council or committee meetings, all of which are costly matters, springs from their desire to fill information gaps about multinational enterprises, financial and labour-wise.

A recent study of multinational unionism by Lloyd Ulman stresses this informational aspect of the unions transnational co-operation. He points out that "A request by a union to the management of a particular subsidiary for information about conditions negotiated or prevailing in other subsidiaries" is usually "rejected on the grounds that each subsidiary is possessed of its own corporate identity and enjoys managerial autonomy". Ulman adds that "the monopoly of information is one of the most important bases of monopoly power ..." and by limiting information flows, corporations strengthen their market power. To the extent that unionists can co-operate and exchange information across national boundaries, Ulman suggests they can avoid some dependence on management.[4]

How such transnational information can become a bargaining counter is revealed in a 1971 report by the Chairman of the British unions' Joint Negotiating Committee which deals with the Ford Motor Company in that country. He stresses "the need for constant touch between different unions particularly among the multinational corporations ...". In this report he went on to "extend my grateful thanks to the prompt information given to us by IG Metall [German metalworkers' union] relative to the settlement at Cologne with Ford ...". He added that in their own negotiation with British Ford, "it gave us considerable pride indeed to be able to tell the Ford Motor Company ... that we had considerable detail of the settlement they had arrived at with IG Metall ..." just a short time before the British Ford negotiations had begun.[5]

A further example of how information can be an important transnational force in labour relations is provided in an earlier example involving the US-based United Automobile Workers and the IMF affiliate in Belgium. The latter, in the late fifties, was confronted with the management of a US auto subsidiary plant in Antwerp which was refusing to grant a year-end bonus. According to the Belgian union the reason given was that "management at Detroit was officially opposed to year-end bonuses". Appraised of the difficulty, and with the threat of a strike at Antwerp,

----

[1] Ibid., passim.

[2] Ibid., p. 9.

[3] Ibid., p. 10.

[4] Lloyd Ulman, "Multinational Unionism: Incentives, Barriers and Alternatives", Industrial Relations (Berkeley), Vol. XIV, No. 1, February 1975, p. 9.

[5] Quoted from E.M. Kassalow, "The International Metalworkers' Federation and the Multinational Automobile Companies", op. cit., p. 270.

the UAW made an intervention in Detroit, and was able to determine that in some plants of the company year-end bonuses were part of workers' compensation. This information was transmitted to the Belgian union. New signals, according to union reports, were subseguqnelty dispatched to the Belgian plant management and a year-end bonus was finally negotiated.[1]

In recent years, the UAW bargaining with Ford, General Motors and Chrysler made use of information on certain working conditions in Europe. Thus, in bargaining for limits on management's right to schedule overtime work in North American plants, the UAW cited already existing union restraints on such management rights in some West European plants of the same companies. Similar use of West European practices was made in negotiating improved relief periods.

The unions' demand for more and better information about the company has almost always been one of the first items set forth during those infrequent meetings when central headquarters officials of a multinational enterprise have met unions on a transnational basis.

Transnational union solidarity and multinationals

Given the rather limited development to date of transnational union-management relations, it is not surprising that there have only been a limited number of cases wherein sympathetic supportive action has been taken by unions at a multinational plant in one country to help a union in another country bargaining with the same enterprise. There is one broad exception to this general absence of transnational supportive action. This has been the substantial number of cases in which unions have expressed dissatisfaction to managers of multinational enterprises with whcm they bargain directly because of the treatment being accorded to workers bargaining with the same company's plant in another country. It might be added that unions surveyed in this report were almost unanimous in their willingness to undertake this type of supportive action.

One of the solidarity tactics vis-à-vis multinational enterprises which has undergone considerable discussion within some of the ITSs has been the willingness and/or ability of unions to refuse to perform overtime work, or at least any new, extra overtime work, when unions at the same company's plant in another country are on strike. The purpose of such a refusal to work overtime is, of course, to prevent the company from making up any lost production.

A very large majority of trade unionists quizzed on this possibility of refusing overtime indicated they would, subject to the approval of their membership, render such support. A few union leaders, especially among those surveyed in the Federal Republic of Germany and the Netherlands, while sympathetic to such a move, indicated they might have difficulty even in presenting such a proposal to their members, under existing collective agreements and labour laws.[2]

A similar very large majority of trade unionists expressed their support cf another solidarity tactic which has been under discussion in some ITSs, namely the willingness to refuse to work on any "struck" production - that is producticn shipped in from a plant of the same multinational in another country which was being struck. Again in a few instances in the Netherlands and the Federal Republic cf Germany some trade union leaders were uncertain as to the legal restraints which might block their rendering such solidarity assistance.

During the course of discussion of the solidarity issues, several trade unionists in most of the countries surveyed volunteered the comment that they would in justifiable cases be prepared even to recommend sympathetic strike action at their own subsidiary plant, to support a union on strike at a plant of the same multinational enterprise in another country.
----

[1] IMF, Résumé des débats de la 4e Conférence internationale de l'automobile, Paris, 28-30 November 1960 (mimeographed), p. 38. This "incident" was also discussed with some of the trade unionists involved in the case.

[2] The subject of the national legal or other limits, country by country, cn transnational union solidarity strike actions is a very complex one. It will be the subject of a forthcoming ILO study, and for this reason no attempt is made to deal with it as such in this report.

In a few cases trade unionists indicated they were not certain they could persuade their members to engage in either of the two types of solidarity referred to above. They indicated their own members rarely struck themselves and might not be sympathetic to supporting a strike of workers, even at the same company, in another country.

One of the important obstacles to the development of such transnational solidarity was the simple lack of contact with and information about unions bargaining with the same multinational in other countries. In one of the relatively few cases where unions have held regular meetings with the management of a multinational company on a transnational basis, the union leaders stated that one important by-product was the way in which it enabled them to establsih relations with unions in other countries bargaining with the same company. Indeed, one leader who has participated in and reported to his members on these transnational union-company meetings declared he was now quite confident he could muster effective solidarity support among his own members, if a strike broke out at the same company's plant in another country.

The various company council or committee meetings called by international trade secretariats or other bodies to bring together union representatives from the same company operating in different countries also helped build such solidarity possibilities. While these meetings received warm endorsement by practically all of the unionists who had participated in them, a few felt that such meetings could be improved by having greater representation by workers from plants of multinational enterprises. In some cases those who attended the meetings were from national union headquarters and they are not always closely informed on plant-level conditions.

As has been previously observed, a central purpose of such transnational union meetings is to exchange and accumulate information about particular multinational enterprises. This accumulation in turn permits ITSs and individual unions to carry on various information and public relations activities vis-à-vis individual multinational companies. Effective public relations action is, at the present time, one of the important union tactics in any disputes they may have with multinationals. The somewhat "exposed" nature of some of these companies, operating as they do in "foreign" environments can make them particularly sensitive to adverse publicity.

Discussion with trade unionists of possible transnational solidarity action against multinationals is handicapped by the oft-times "hypothetical" nature of the issue. Thus, any possible substantial sympathetic action might well depend upon the actual details of the case for which sympathetic support was being sought, and the condition of the labour market when such support was being solicited.

As a matter of general solidarity, practically all unionists surveyed expressed warm support for the view that at least certain basic minimum labour standards should be required of multinationals, regardless of where they were operating. These include the recognition of unions at their various plants. Many trade unionists also believed that certain basic minimum working conditions should be guaranteed by a multinational employer, regardless of where its plants were located.

Employers' views on development of
transnational labour relations

While the unions generally seem quite favourable to the development of at least some forms of transnational labour relations and meetings with top management of multinational enterprises, the companies generally express opposition to such developments. As regards the "practicability of international collective bargaining", according to the survey made by the International Organisation of Employers (IOE), companies feel this would be "completely impracticable and morecver undesirable". The IOE report mentions such problems as: who would represent the employees, this often being difficult enough to sort out at a national level; the fact that the present trend for greater employee participation and plant bargaining runs against such transnational proposals; the fact that such transnationalism would work against the delegation of collective bargaining power to subsidiaries;

the erosion of the power of national and industry employer associations; and the weakening of direct company-union and employee relations.[1]

The director of personnel of the Philips company also sees the trend toward greater shop floor demands in bargaining as an obstacle to trade union demands for more transnational bargaining, especially in Europe.[2]

Legal restraints on transnational labour developments

Generally speaking, officials of European employers' associations stress the great differences in legal systems when the subject of transnational bargaining is under consideration. In the Federal Republic of Germany, for example, where so large a part of labour conditions in a given plant is regulated by national law, it was viewed as impossible to foresee collective bargaining with multinational enterprises that would embrace German members and plants with others which operated in countries where laws and collective agreements were so different.

Additionally, in terms of the legal aspects of the labour policies of multinational companies, a number of employer association spokesmen in Western Europe believe it would be impractical and unfair to impose on multinational companies special rules that went beyond the requirements for national companies.

Employer views on locus of decision making in bargaining

Employer spokesmen strongly insist that the determination of employment conditions is essentially a matter of local decision making. It is argued that this applies to multinational plants as well as to national companies with the possible exception of one or two items such as pensions in the case of multinational companies.

To the charge sometimes voiced by unions that the home offices of multi-national companies dictate "centrally wage bargaining procedures and industrial relations policy", the Shell International Petroleum Company, for example, has responded that employment conditions are "essentially matters which must be shaped by the environment in which a company works ...". Shell policy and practice is that the "level and conditions of employment are determined by national companies within their own national setting ...".[3]

A number of employers' organisations did indicate that decisions on pension programmes of multinational subsidiaries, some of which had been instituted voluntarily by the companies in the first instance, are sometimes an exception to the general policy of decentralisation. Major changes in such programmes often had to be made in consultation with a company's home offices.

Some management spokesmen have pointed to the contradiction inherent in the demands of unions that on the one hand multinational companies should conform to local national customs in bargaining and on the other hand the demands of some unions that these companies should also engage in forms of transnational bargaining. A top executive of the Nestlé Company has called attention to the possible contradiction in these two kinds of demands. He states that the call for a policy
----

[1] IOE, op. cit., p. 27.

[2] P.L. Dronkers, "A multinational organisation and industrial relations: The Philips case", paper presented to the Third World Congress, International Industrial Relations Association, London, England, 3-7 September 1973, p. 4. He writes: "The fact that trade unions generally, in formulating demands in conditions of employment, are basing themselves increasingly on the shop floor (which has not made the position of the national union federations any easier), has not promoted the 'convergence' at a European level either."

[3] Shell International Company, "Multinational Enterprise" (London, presumably 1973), p. 8. This is a statement apparently prepared for submission to the United Nations Eminent Persons Inquiry into Multinationals, but it was not published in those proceedings.

of decentralisation which "makes firms as autonomous and as national as possble" is incompatible with the kind of centralisation policy which would be "necessary for any possible dialogue with international trade unions."[1] The same Nestlé executive also raises a question as to who would be the appropriate international trade union representatives for such a dialogue, since "The national trade unions' claim to be the only interlocutors on problems concerning their countries."[2]

An executive of the Ford Motor Company has similarly written that "so far we have not perceived any willingness of the employees of one Ford national company to identify their interests closely enough with employees of another national Ford Company so as to cause any kind of concerted action between the two groups of employees", which would "be intended to prompt the managers to take a particular course of action."[3]

A Swedish employers' association executive also voiced the view that in their experience, if anything, national trade union leaders were more "nationally" minded than managers and he doubted that union leaders were ready for genuinely international forms of labour relations.

Multinationals and international consultation with unions

The International Organisation of Employers' survey of social policies and practices of multinational companies does not deal specifically with proposals for transnational consultation with unions, but only sets out company attitudes on transnational bargaining. A survey of British multinational enterprises which also found strong company opposition to forms of transnational forms of bargaining, found considerably less opposition to the possibility of "union-management consultative meetings on a regional or international basis".[4]

During the course of this ILO survey several individual employer representatives seemed to indicate there could be some value in union-management consultations at a transnational level. These should, however, they felt, be largely of an informational nature. Some company officials expressed the fear that unions might try to escalate such consultation into bargaining sessions.[5] Related to this fear was the feeling that unions might exploit the meetings via excessive public reports on them.

Roberts and May's study of British-based multinational enterprises indicates that of those replying to a questionnaire, some 37 per cent indicated that they would "co-operate" or "reluctantly co-operate" with union requests for "meetings on a regional or international basis". Twenty-six per cent would "neither hinder nor help" and 37 per cent would engage in "resistance" or "determined resistance" in such requests. A somewhat similar survey of US-based multinational enterprises by David Blake showed 75 per cent of the companies prepared for "determined resistance"

----

[1] Statement of Pierre Liotard-Vogt in United Nations, Hearings before the Group of Eminent Persons, op. cit., p. 284.

[2] Ibid.

[3] Robert Copp, "The Labour Affairs Function in a Multinational Firm", Industrial Relations Association, Spring Meeting, Jamaica, 3-6 May 1973 (Madison, Wisconsin, IRRA, 1973), p. 457.

[4] Roberts and May, op. cit., p. 411. These two authors found that only 24 per cent of the British multinationals surveyed either were neutral with regard to bargaining transnationally, or considered that it might be "helpful" in 4 per cent of the cases. On the other hand as regards "union-management consultation meetings on a regional or international basis" 50 per cent were either neutral towards or felt these might be "helpful"; the other 50 per cent indicated they thought such proposals for transnational consultation were "harmful".

[5] On the distinction between "consultation" and "negotiation" in this context, the Federation of Swedish Industries, op. cit., p. 19, notes that some unions have formed "groups to keep a watch" on "certain multinational companies". It adds: "more and more companies have also shown themselves eager to collaborate with such committees. It is seldom that more concrete negotiations take place however."

or "resistance" to such a request by unions, with only 4 per cent ready to co-operate, and 21 per cent neither hindering or helping.[1]

----

[1] Roberts and May, op. cit., p. 412; Blake, op. cit., p. 247.

CHAPTER VII

COMPANY-UNION TRANSNATIONAL MEETINGS AND CONTACTS

The number of meetings which have been held to date between multinational enterprises and representatives of their workers, on a union-company transnational basis, has been quite limited. The number of union requests for full-scale meetings of this type has actually not been as great as might be imagined. There should be no confusion between transnational union meetings involving workers from the same company as opposed to meetings between the same unions and multinational enterprises. Quite frequently even when unions have held such transnational meetings of their own convened, for example, either by an international trade secretariat or by a group of shop stewards acting on their own, these have not been followed by requests for a meeting with the same multinational company.

Examples of company-union
transnational meetings

Among the more interesting of these transnational-union-management experiences has been that involving the Philips Company of the Netherlands and a number of West European unions which bargain with it in various countries on a national basis. Some four meetings were held over several years between this company and the unions, the last one in 1972. The relationship was suspended in 1973 for several reasons. There seemed to be some fear on the company's part that the unions were seeking to push the discussions from a consultative to a bargaining type of relation, particularly as concerned proposals for greater employment and related income security. The company also objected to the position of the unions that it was "necessary that a representative of the International Metalworkers' Federation (IMF) attend a proposed fifth meeting as an observer".[1]

After a lapse of several years a new effort was made by the unions and the Philips management to resume these meetings. Once again, however, it seems to have failed at the very last moment because of the company's objections to the inclusion of an IMF observer among the union delegation. The unions took the position that the nature of the agreed-upon agenda made it essential for this observer from the IMF to be present. On the agenda was an item which involved "survey of Philips on the social and economic development of the European Community vis-à-vis the world and consequences for Philips". The unions also took the position that they had the exclusive right to name their "own representatives, in exactly the same way as that the company management uses this right to name its representative".[2]

The same problem of which representatives of workers may attend transnational meetings with management also proved difficult, for a short time, in a case involving a relatively small German-Dutch multinational in the transportation equipment industry. Here the company meets regularly every six months with workers'
----

[1] Dronkers (of the Philips Company), op. cit., p. 4. For a union viewpoint of the experience see the chapter by Günter Köpke (of the European Metalworkers' Federation) in Flanagan and Weber, op. cit., pp. 212-213. A useful survey of the Philips meeting to date can be found in European Industrial Relations Review, Preview Issue, (London, 1974).

[2] European Metalworkers' Federation in the Community, Press Release, 30 May 1975, Eindhoven. (The European Metalworkers' Federation (EMF) has acted as co-ordinating body for the unions and has participated in all these meetings with Philips. The IMF has a close relationship with the EMF, and most of the unions affiliated to the latter also belong to the IMF). The IMF General Secretary sharply criticised "Philips attitude", declaring "that the choice of who should take part in a trade union delegation is a basic trade union right, and one which we shall guard jealously". IMF, Press Release, 4 June 1975, Geneva. The company's position is that the original framework of the meetings was the European Economic Community, and this should not include any representative of the IMF. Dronkers, op. cit., p. 4. When there was disagreement over the May 1975 meeting, the company held to its position that the framework of the meetings was the EEC, and it offered to meet with union representatives from EEC countries (including the EMF), without the participation of the IMF representative, but the unions refused.

representatives from its several plants in the Federal Republic of Germany and the Netherlands. In between the regular meetings a small group of plant representatives hammers out an agenda for the semi-annual meeting. This transnational relationship dates back to 1970.

At an early stage in these transnational relations the issue of who could attend the meetings arose. The company at one point challenged the workers' delegation when it included an officer from the European Metalworkers' Federation, presumably on the grounds that he was not a company employee.

The solution that was worked out seems, in effect, to concede that while the company is meeting with the workers' representatives from its own plants, the workers can include other individuals of their choice in making up their representation. This has been accomplished by an exchange of memoranda.

For these meetings the company bears the expenses of any workers coming directly from the plant; the various unions pay the expenses of their representatives. High on the agenda of the meetings have been what union representatives describe as very full and candid reports by the company on its investment, production and employment plans and prospects. The very forthcoming position of the company on these matters has helped to create a favourable environment for co-operation between the parties.

Among the issues that have come before the parties at their meetings, employment problems have been prominent. As it happens, in one year the Dutch plants had a surplus of workers, and it was agreed that rather than lay them off they should be transferred to the Federal Republic of Germany branch. More recently the German plants facing a labour surplus transferred workers to the Netherlands. As employment prospects have continued to be somewhat poor at the German plants, it was agreed to inscribe on the agenda for the next semi-annual meeting between all parties the possibility of transferring work from the Netherlands to the Federal Republic of Germany.

As well as trying to deal with employment surpluses or shortages, the workers' side has also raised the issue of extending or harmonising some general practices of employment security. In this case it appeared that Dutch laws and related bargaining arrangements were superior to those in the Federal Republic of Germany. The company took the position that they could hardly agree to let the unions "pick the raisins out of the cake." In other words various benefits were part of a total and had to be evaluated as a whole in comparing conditions between one country and another, and merely to select one superior benefit for wider application was unreasonable. The issue is still under discussion.[1]

It seemed to be recognised in this German-Dutch case that different laws, bargaining structures and the like made full joint bargaining a very doubtful matter. On the other hand, some of the Dutch unions (there are three different Dutch national unions involved) in the course of these meetings seemed to develop an interest in exploring the possibility of their having a voice on the supervisory board of the company's central control office which is situated in the Federal Republic of Germany. As it happens this international company office which stands above the Dutch and German branches is of a relatively small size and it therefore does not come under the law of the Federal Republic of Germany which provides for worker representation on some company supervisory boards. Thus German, let alone Dutch workers, are not represented on the international company's supervisory board.[2]

----

[1] The question of a generally upward harmonised employment security plan was also one of the specific demands advanced by the unions in some of the Philips meetings referred to above.

[2] Following the absorption of part of the Dutch car company DAF by the Swedish Volvo Company, it was reported that one Dutch union had immediately raised the possibility of having a union representative on the Board of the DAF company. This was apparently prompted by the fact that Swedish unions are represented on the Volvo Board. This Dutch union felt that such a new union board member could "deal specially with continuity of full employment"; this reflected fears of possible layoffs resulting from the merger. See IMF, Release from the World Auto Councils, 25 September, 1974.

Another transnational-company-union relationship which seems to shcw possibilities of continuity is that between Rothmans International and a group of tobacco workers' unions affiliated to the International Union of Food and Allied Workers' Associations (IUF). This company is a division of the Rupert-Rembrandt group, a South African-based tobacco and beverage company.

At a meeting held in February, 1974, union representatives (from IUF affiliates in Belgium, the Federal Republic of Germany, Netherlands and the United Kingdom, as well as representatives from the IUF headquarters) and company representatives (Rothmans' Managing Director and two of his assistants) attended. The unions stressed their great interest in the firm's long-term investment plans particularly as regards the reallocation or transfers of production. Moreover, the union representatives indicated they were not opposed to new investment or the installation of new machinery, but they wanted to be consulted in advance of such moves. The company stated it was not aware of cases where new machinery had been installed without prior consultation with unions. The unions pressed to be consulted on the company's longer term planning, and the management indicated that it would take this under consideration with its Board. The meeting was cordial and the parties agreed to meet again in 1975.[1]

There are of course some other examples of transnational meetings between multinational enterprises and union representatives in the industries covered by this survey. Most of these, however, have only consisted of a single meeting and have not involved significant continuity in union-management transnational relations.

Meetings between IMF affiliated unions and the automobile companies have generally been of this one-time nature; but there have been two transnational meetings with the Ford Motor Company.

During the course of its world auto councils' conference in Detroit, in 1966, the IMF requested meetings with the major United States auto companies, and Ford and General Motors agreed. At the Ford meeting the unions from less-developed countries took the opportunity to indicate some of their difficulties. A delegate frcm Argentina, for example, claimed that in a "recent strike" local management had threatened to close down the plant. Ford management claimed to have no knowledge of the incident, and stressed that they deferred to local, subsidiary plant managers on labour matters. The IMF Conference noted that meetings such as these "were not collective bargaining sessions as such ...." but delegates were able to make known serious problems to top management, a rare opportunity for most of them.[2]

At an IMF European Regional Meeting of Ford workers in 1972, Moss Evans, representative of the British Transport and General Workers' Union, which among the 20 odd British unions recognised by Ford represents by far the largest number of workers in that company, took the lead in pressing for a European-wide Ford union-management conference.[3] Despite efforts which included some pressure on their own managements by other unions at Ford plants in Europe, the request was turned down.

Evans strongly believed that the development of a comprehensive European production strategy on the part of Ford necessitated a common European approach to the Company. Such a union strategy, he argued, would prevent the company frcm threatening "that whole manufacturing operations will be transferred from one ccuntry to another".[4]

In turning down the proposal of the IMF the company indicated that it felt that no useful purpose could be served by such a meeting. According to union
----

[1] IUF, Documents of the Secretariat Executive Committee, 28-30 January 1975, item II. The present report is based on this document as well as conversations with IUF officials who participated in it.

[2] IMF, Report of the First International Conference World Auto Councils, Detroit, Michigan, 31 May-3 June 1966, p. 63.

[3] For the unions' reasons behind this move see E.M. Kassalow: "The International Metalworkers' Federation and the Multinational Automobile Companies", op. cit., p. 64.

[4] On the special concern of British unions about such possible Ford production facility transfers see Ibid.

sources a company spokesman argued that labour laws and bargaining procedures differed from country to country, and, moreover, local managers were empowered to make all necessary decisions.

IMF with strong support from its North American affiliate the United Automobile Workers (UAW) continued to press Ford for a meeting. Finally, the company did agree to meet in Detroit on 9 February 1973 with a delegation that consisted of UAW and IMF representatives. For the company the vice-president for labour relations and two of his colleagues who worked for Ford on labour matters on the international level were present.[1]

The union delegation pointed out that Ford had already met, in Detroit in 1966, with Ford union representatives from seven countries. Union representatives also noted that a number of European countries were meeting on a European basis with union delegations (Philips, Brown Boveri and Nestlé were noted). The union side argued that both groups would gain from periodic world-wide meetings which would improve communications.

Company representatives reiterated their position that differences in labour law and practices made inter-country level meetings inadvisable.

In countering this argument the union participants stated that Ford's "policies regarding production, planning and investment affecting the jobs and security of our members, were based on a purely global approach".

The company agreed to consider all points raised and indicated that if any reply were made it would be through the UAW. It seems clear that although the Company had agreed to meet with a joint UAW-IMF delegation, it was being quite cautious about extending recognition to IMF. It is likely that both in the 1966 and 1973 meetings the company was responding especially to pressures from the UAW.

*   *   *

In general it can be said that much emphasis in meetings of these types is placed by the participating unions on employment and related production and investment questions. Some complaints are frequently made about "mistreatment" of unions by specific subsidiary management at particular plants, usually in less developed countries, particularly as regards union recognition or treatment of union representatives. On occasion some general problems relating to conditions of work may also be raised, for example, the "safety" factors involved in handling certain materials. The unions may also press for some uniform standards to be applied throughout the company to improve safety in such cases.

The lack of continuity as regards many such meetings makes it somewhat difficult to judge their possible substantive direction.

A recent development on the unions' side suggests one limited way of their getting around objections of multinational top management to their meeting with other than their home country unions. In the United States, some of the IMF affiliates which bargain with multinationals have, in a few cases, invited representatives from IMF affiliates overseas to attend at least the opening sessions of their bargaining with some multinational enterprises. This invitation is naturally limited to affiliates which bargain overseas with subsidiaries of the same company. Conversations with some of those trade unionists from Western Europe who have participated in such sessions indicate it to have been a useful experience. One Belgian unionist who sat in on negotiations between the Caterpillar Company and the United Automobile Workers stated that he gained insights into the way in which grievances were handled and contracts were negotiated.[2] Without necessarily being in

----

[1] This account is based primarily on IMF release from the IMF World Auto Councils, 13 February 1973, re: Meeting of the IMF Representatives with the Ford Motor Company in the United States of America. The company has not issued a release for this meeting.

[2] The foreign union participants in their negotiations with Caterpillar are listed in UAW, News from UAW, 6 July 1973. Included were representatives from Belgium, the Federal Republic of Germany, the United Kingdom, France and an official of the IMF. (See also IMF, News No. 29, July 1973).

full agreement with the different procedures he observed, he was better able, thereafter, to comprehend some of the same company's labour relations practices in his own country. A trade unionist from the Federal Republic of Germany had similar reactions.

It is not clear how far the few experiences of this sort, to date, which have been undertaken by the UAW and IMF may be extended. It is possible that in some countries legal obstacles could prevent home country unions from bringing foreign country unionists into negotiations, as part of their delegation.

Union intervention with multinationals to assist workers in other countries

Among the most significant transnational types of pressures which unions can bring to bear against a multinational company are those which can be exercised on behalf of workers who are encountering difficulties with the same company's subsidiary in another country. These kinds of actions are often co-ordinated by the various international trade union secretariats; they are also often led by unions in the home country of the enterprise.

There have been many cases of this type. Just recently, for example, when the General Motors Corporation announced it was planning to shut down operations in its Bienne, Switzerland Plant, the IMF Automotive Department alerted "all members of the [IMF] General Motors World Auto Council, particularly the United Automobile Workers ...." in the United States. IMF charged that the company's decision to close the plant was taken without the advance notice which was called for in the collective agreement. Some 1,000 workers in the small town of Bienne were said to be affected by this announcement.

The vice-president of the UAW in charge of that union's large General Motors Department in the United States and Canada wrote "a forceful letter to the Chairman of the Board" of the Corporation, in which he "requested further consideration of the company's decision" and also "suggested a meeting of the Swiss Metalworkers' Federation and the Directors of the company's overseas division".[1]

A number of cases involving metalworkers in Spain have, in recent years, led to strong home country intervention on the part of other metal-working unions in Western Europe. A series of partial strikes and lockouts at the SKF company Madrid plant in October 1973, led the Swedish metalworkers union (SKF has its headquarters in Sweden) to intervene with top management, especially after the company dismissed a number of workers at its Madrid plant. The total dismissed reached 60 at one point, the union charged. The Swedish metalworkers "protested vigorously" to home company management, and also issued a public appeal on behalf of the Spanish workers. The latter were also "backed by the national shop stewards and works council conference of the German metalworkers' union" and by "the distribution of 6,000 leaflets at SKF plants in Italy". Protests were also made to SKF plant management in France by IMF affiliates in that country. The company eventually rehired all but four of the workers, according to union sources.[2] The very strong position of the Swedish metalworkers at SKF home country operations was probably the most critical union force in this case.

During the course of a 37-day strike at a British Leyland Motors Corporation plant in Pamplona, Spain, British metal unions intervened especially on behalf of those workers who had been discharged and placed on the "local black list". According to IMF reports, other protests were made, through the IMF - BLMC World Council, to company managers in the United Kingdom, India, Bangladesh and New Zealand.[3]

In another case involving the French automobile producer Renault local unionists from the Confédération Générale du Travail (CGT) and the Confédération

----

[1] IMF, News, No. 10, June 1975.

[2] IMF, News, No. 4, October, 1973.

[3] IMF, Release from the IMF World Auto Councils, "Details of the end of the Authi (BLMC) strike in Spain", 14 July 1974. According to this report the discharged workers "had their names removed from the 'local black list' and will be given employment in Pamplona ...".

Française Démocratique du Travail (CFDT) protested strongly against the company's alleged actions in violating workers' rights in a Spanish plant. According to the unionists some five worker delegates had been laid off at the Renault plant in Valladolid, Spain, and another 56 had been "sanctioned" in a conflict involving workers' rights of representation. The French workers demanded a cancellation of the layoffs and the sanctions.[1]

Pressure on behalf of a transnational labour objective was also brought to bear by French unions in a September 1968 case involving the Peugeot company. The Argentine union Sindicato de Mecánicos y Afines de Transporte Automotor (SMATA) appealed to the IMF during the course of a difficult strike with that company's subsidiary plant in Argentina. A number of workers had been fired and many more suspended by the company.

The IMF appealed to its French affiliates and the latter along with the CGT, not affiliated to the IMF, protested to home company management. They distributed a large number of leaflets on the strike in the home company plants and also threatened a 15 minute demonstration strike in support of the Argentine union and its members. The strike was finally settled in Argentina and the workers who had been suspended and discharged were re-employed according to the IMF report.

The International Union of Food and Allied Workers' Associations reported that when one of its US-Canadian affiliates went on strike against 13 plants of the Nabisco company in September 1969, it alerted its affiliates in 10 countries where the company was known to have its subsidiaries, and requested these affiliates to convey to their own local managements their support of the strike. This was done, IUF reports, in seven countries. Three Italian food unions (two of them IUF affiliates) staged a one-hour sympathy strike at the Genoa and Milan plants of the company. The strike was settled the following month, and the United States union expressed its thanks to the IUF.[2]

At the request of an Italian affiliate which bargains with Coca Cola in Italy, the IUF requested affiliates to support Italian unions which were protesting against the closing of a Coca Cola plant in Rome in 1971. Affiliates from some 11 countries are reported to have indicated their support by intervening with management at their own Coca Cola plants. The IUF Danish food affiliate sent financial aid to the workers. Food unions affiliated to the French CGT and the Hungarian union trade centre, neither affiliated to the IUF, are also reported to have indicated their support of the Italian strikers. The IUF adds that after some drawn out negotiations, with the help of intervention by the Italian government most of the jobs affected were saved.[3]

There are, of course, also cases of union intervention which are less organised in character. Shop stewards in subsidiary plants in one country may be contacted by those on strike or in difficulty at the same company's plant in another country. The stewards in the country contacted by the strikers may thereupon express their concern to their own management. These cases also occur with some frequency, but are harder to document as to the steps taken and the issues involved. Cases of bilateral or trilateral national union contacts vis-à-vis multinational enterprises have also occurred without the intervention of any international trade union secretariat.

It is difficult to estimate the direct outcome or effects of these types of interventions by unions with their own managements on behalf of unions in another country. Management of multinationals will generally insist that any subsequent actions or strike settlements which were forthcoming were not due to the transnational union pressures. The unions may make the contrary claim, or at least insist such pressures were one element influencing management's attitude.
----

[1] The preparation of and dispatch of the protest letter was one of the actions growing out of a conference of Renault trade unionists held in Paris, 29 January-1 February 1974. See Conference Internationale Des Travailleurs du Groupe Renault (no date, or place of publication indicated).

[2] IUF, 16th Congress, Zurich, 7-10 July (Geneva, 1970), "Other Activities", p. 2.

[3] IUF, 17th Congress, Geneva, 23 January-2 February 1973 (Geneva, 1973), V-8, pp. 14-15.

Clearly, however, this is one of the tools or weapons most extensively used by unions when difficulties occur in one or several plants of a multinational. Such a tool is transnational in character though it does not involve direct relations of the unions of a multinational company with management of that company.

The effectiveness of this type of intervention often depends heavily upon the strength of the union which bargains with the multinational in the home country. If this union enjoys a strong and effective relationship with the company, the latter is likely to be more sensitive to pressures like these.

In any event this form of transnational action is certain to continue to be an important part of union and management relations in multinational enterprises.

Not all cases of transnational union action vis-à-vis multinationals in a single country have a "conflictive" setting. One North American union, the International Union of Electrical Radio and Machine Workers (IUE) was experiencing serious difficulties in 1974 with a subsidiary plant of a Belgian metals company, Bekaert SA. Not long after the latter had opened a plant in one of the southern states in the United States, a severe strike occurred before the IUE could achieve recognition and its first collective agreement with the subsidiary. Relations between the parties had continued poorly thereafter.

Some months later, when a top IUE official was in Belgium at the request of the IMF, the latter's Belgian affiliate which enjoyed a good relationship with the same company arranged a meeting between the United States union official and Bekaert's top management. According to union reports the meeting was very cordial and constructive, and the company indicated its desire to place relationships with the IUE on a new and improved footing.[1]

The Swedish electrical manufacturing company LM Ericsson, according to a European labour relations newsletter, has made funds available "to permit union representatives of its various plants around the world to visit one another".[2]

The same newsletter reports that the United States-based Budd Manufacturing corporation "invited representatives of the United Automobile Workers to join management on a 10-day tour of automotive plants in five European countries", in 1973.[3]

There are, of course, other examples of peaceful transnational co-operation between some unions and multinational enterprises in different countries.

Company-union relations, growth
in transnationalism

Whether through meetings with a group of unions from their plants in different countries, by pressures of individual unions on individual plant managers designed to achieve transnational objectives, or merely as a result of joint meetings between unions bargaining with the same company in different countries for the purpose of pooling information and co-ordinating strategy even in the absence of a common meeting with the same company, a number of multinationals seem increasingly to be subjected to transnational union pressures.

A very recent study of The Conference Board reports that among 134 United States-based multinational companies with a significant proportion of blue-collar workers represented by unions at their subsidiaries, 10 per cent had already had "action against them taken across national frontiers" by unions. Another 14 per cent "reported that unionised company employees had undertaken multinational actions
----

[1] This account is based on IMF, News, No. 35, November 1974, as well as conversations with some of the trade unionists from both countries and the IMF who participated in the meeting.

[2] Industrial Relations Europe, Newsletter (Brussels), September 1974. The Swedish metalworkers' union confirms this arrangement; the arrangement, however, does not provide for any group or central meeting of LM Ericsson union delegates from different plants around the world.

[3] Ibid.

among themselves, short of actual contacts with management". Of 34 multinational enterprises based outside the United States the Conference Board report indicates that 21 per cent had "experienced multinational union contacts" and 24 per cent "reported purely intra-union actions which had not yet developed into contacts with management".[1]

All this suggests that a trend towards transnational dealings is gradually taking shape in a number of countries, though the process is slow and is likely to be influenced by a number of different forces.

----

[1] The Conference Board, op. cit., p. 9. As previously observed fn. 1 p. 88, above, it is difficult to evaluate precisely the meaning of some of the responses in questionnaire surveys such as these. If a large company with many subsidiary plants abroad had experienced "multinational union action" at a few of these plants, presumably the company as a whole would fall into the "class" of those which had undergone such experience. The data nevertheless are an interesting indicator of the substantial growth in multinational labour actions.

CHAPTER VIII

MAJOR FINDINGS AND CONCLUSIONS

For the most part the industrial relations systems of West European countries have absorbed or assimilated the subsidiary plants of multinational enterprises in the food and metal industries which have been established in these countries. To put it another way, for the most part, multinational plants operating in Western European countries have adapted, or had to adapt to host country labour practices. But while there has been this general absorption or adaptation, there are important exceptions to this process of assimilation as regards a variety of labour practices in every one of the countries studied. So much so, that often the exception and variation introduced in labour practices of multinational subsidiaries seem at least as important to unions as does the general, over-all assimilation of these companies. Furthermore, in a few countries the multinationals' special labour practices have had general influence on national labour practices, and this is especially true in some industries.

The importance attached by unions to these variations and exceptions is attested to by the volume of speeches, meetings and declarations about multinational companies which so many unions and union leaders have been party to in recent years.[1]

Moreover, with regard to at least one important general aspect of the multinationals' impact, a large majority of trade unionists everywhere express concern and the need for further action of a transnational nature. Reference is made here to the related issues of employment security and company investment and employment policies in foreign-owned multinational plants in Western Europe. The unions' desire for an opportunity to have a more direct impact into home country, company headquarters' decisions in these matters is broadly characteristic, regardless of country or industry. This seems to have its origin in the fact that for multinationals generally, regardless of type of industry or the country of origin, critical investment allocations which may substantially affect production and employment are primarily a central, home office function.

While the growth of company-union transnational meetings has been a slow process, many such companies are experiencing other forms of transnational union pressures. A great majority of such companies are strongly opposed to the idea of transnational collective bargaining, but a number seem less opposed to some form of transnational consultation with unions.

National differences in reactions
to multinationals

Again while one can speak of the general absorption of multinationals, there are important differences between countries. The national industrial relations structures of some countries are far more constraining of multinational companies' labour practices than is the case of others. The manner in which, for example, so much of the substance and structure of labour-management relations is prescribed by law in a country like the Federal Republic of Germany, as compared to a more voluntaristic system like that in the United Kingdom, almost inevitably ensures greater conformity by multinationals to national practices in the former as opposed to the latter country.

The strength and character of union and management associations in one country as compared to another, can act as an intervening modifier of industrial relations

----

[1] At its 1974 Congress, the General Secretary of the International Metalworkers' Federation observed that over one-third of that body's meetings in 1973 were directed at multinational company problems. Almost every speaker, representing his own national union at this major international gathering of metal-working unions, at least in the opening round of addresses included significant reference to and criticism of these same companies. Of course many of these criticisms of multinationals are directed at their general economic policies and influence, and not only at their labour practices. IMF, Proceedings of the Twenty-Third Congress, Stockholm, 2-6 July 1974 (Geneva: 1974) p. 15 et seq.

conduct in multinational enterprises. Thus, in Sweden where the formal, legal industrial relations constraints on practices in a multinational subsidiary may not be as significant as in the Federal Republic of Germany, the great strength of union and management federations and the structure of their joint relations result in a high degree of "conformity" on the part of multinational companies.

Another element which affects the assimilation of absorption process as regards multinationals' labour practices may be the size of a given country. At least in the case of Belgium and the Netherlands, some of the unions' concern with multinationals seems to be a function of the relatively small size of these countries, as compared, for example, to the Federal Republic of Germany or France. Even a few multinationals which do not conform well to national labour practices, stand out vividly in a small country landscape. Furthermore, even in a larger country the special impact of one or several multinationals in a limited area (frequently a so-called development area) may generate union concern about the labour practices of these companies.

Differences in industrial technology and organisation also seem to be a force influencing the impact of multinationals upon the host country's industrial relations system and the unions therein. Where investment in any given plant and its related equipment is almost inevitably very large, as for example, in the automobile industry, a multinational enterprise is likely to exercise greater influence over a foreign subsidiary including some influence on personnel policies, than might be the case of a company in another industry where the level of investment in a subsidiary is more modest, because of technological factors. Food companies seem to be characterised by somewhat more decentralised policy-making than is the case of automobile companies, to choose two very different types. As a result, the labour problems posed by automobile as against food companies may be different in some respects.

There are, within the intervening variables mentioned in preceding paragraphs, some differences to be found between "old" and "new" multinationals. It is more often the latter which will tend to import their own practices. Even as between newly installed multinationals the geographical area of location may influence some of their labour conduct, particularly in the first few years. Thus in more "integrated" areas, where unions are strong, the multinationals may conform more fully and quickly to national labour-management patterns. On the other hand, a multinational located in a less developed and less well unionised area, may carry in some of its own labour practices, at least for a substantial period of time.

Not only may there be distinctions between old and new multinationals, but there may be distinctions in conduct which can sometimes be traced to their country of origin. The greater distance, for example, between the US-based companies and their subsidiaries, the larger differences between the United States industrial relations system and those of Western Europe in general, the usually greater importance of the United States home market and the highly developed industrial relations practices and offices of US-based companies, may lead some of the latter to exercise closer control over their subsidiaries, and to introduce, consciously or not, more of their home labour practices than is usually the case with European-based multinationals. The special union recognition experience of United States firms, at home, is a good case in point, in evaluating some of their experiences in the United Kingdom. The attitude to strikes of some United States multinationals in Belgium is another instance.

Multinationals, integrated enterprises

Perhaps even more to the point is that many multinationals tend to live in or create a somewhat special world.[1] Their internal communications are more developed; they must be to operate far-flung companies. Their industrial relations functions,

----

[1] What is said here is true, in some respects, of most large, multi-plant companies, regardless of whether they are multinational or not. But national, multi-plant companies have grown up as part of the national industrial relations experience, they are not preoccupied with outside home country fiscal or other relations, they are more likely to be part of national employers' associations and their central offices are immediately accessible to the national unions and to government officials.

especially in the case of United States firms, are often more professionalised. Their fringe benefits and sometimes the wages they pay are often in the lead, compared to surrounding plants in Western Europe. Their systems of personnel training are often more "modern" and developed and more inward based than is the case with most national companies. Their managers may look to home country offices and structures for their wider career aspirations. In some multinationals there appears to be a significant system of rotating managers to different countries, as part of their training and experience. Their wages systems, job evaluation, performance ratings and the like sometimes reflect their long experience elsewhere. Some of them are not accustomed to dealing with employees through employer association-union bargaining (their more professionalised industrial relations functions make this less necessary), and they sometimes avoid such relationships. For some multinationals their home country conceptions of what is the appropriate framework or subject matter for collective bargaining, what should or should not be the nature of strike action, these and other subtle conceptions may influence their labour relations conduct abroad, and can become an irritant or problem for the host country union.

All of these and other factors often tend to make of the multinational a more integrated enterprise, with personnel more specialised and turned inward. One can hardly criticise better fringe benefits or more training, but from a union viewpoint the net result of the foregoing state of affairs, the greater "integration" of multinationals, makes such enterprises more difficult to penetrate in terms of union presence and power in relation to personnel and to management. In some cases, unions are also convinced that the object of this "integration" is to frustrate the impact of the union. In at least one country it is also argued multinationals sometimes afford poorer facilities and accept the union with greater difficulty than is the case with national companies.

The sometimes more "difficult" relationships with multinational enterprises may help explain the general malaise or dissatisfaction that union leaders express vis-à-vis multinationals even when they concede that economic benefits provided by these companies usually, but by no means always compare well with those of comparable national competitors.

The general, widespread and universally-expressed union feeling that it is much more difficult to be well informed about multinational companies, their policies and financial status, adds to this sense of being kept at bay. Inadequate information, in the union view, is a major complaint about multinational companies.

This feeling of being held at arm's length by multinationals, as against a national company, naturally varies from country to country. Certainly in the Federal Republic of Germany where legislation enters very deeply into prescribing the structure of intra-plant worker-manager relations, and employer associations and national unions are very strong, there is less feeling of this than is the case of Belgium or especially the United Kingdom, where the labour relations system is more voluntary in character. Multinationals may, in many ways, constitute less of a distinct problem to unions in France as compared, for example, to Belgium or the United Kingdom, even though the level of unionism is certainly strikingly higher in the latter two countries. The intervening variables of the national industrial relations system, with so much being prescribed by legislation in France may account for this. The size of country (Belgium and France) also comes into play, as does the degree of penetration by multinational companies.

These foregoing general factors which influence the impact or lack of it of multinational enterprises on union-management relations in Western Europe, naturally vary greatly as between different aspects of labour relations. Any special union recognition difficulties, vis-à-vis multinationals, for example, are not likely to occur in France, the Federal Republic of Germany or Belgium, since membership in employers' associations in those countries particularly for larger firms (in a sense, almost all multinationals are large or middle-sized firms) is virtually necessary given those countries' social tradition and administration, and with this membership comes more or less automatic recognition of unions. On the other hand, even though the general level of unionism is higher in the United Kingdom than in the Federal Republic of Germany or France, it is easier in the former for a multinational to avoid joining its "appropriate" employers' association. In this case it may or may not recognise the union, and although it has in most cases, the exceptions are a source of irritation to the labour movement in the United Kingdom and to a degree in the Netherlands. But even in cases where the union has been recognised the greater propensity of multinationals in the United Kingdom to opt out of employer associations (as compared to companies of comparable size, at least in the industries studied here) again tends to set some of them apart somewhat, and at times to make them a special "object" of unions' concern.

Union experience and reactions in collective bargaining with multinationals in Western Europe

In the face of the relatively good economic benefits[1] which workers enjoy at most multinational companies in Western Europe, it is not surprising that most European trade unionists saw no pressing need for the development of full-scale forms of transnational collective bargaining. In some instances this attitude seems to have been influenced by the legal obstacles confronting transnational collective bargaining, such as differences in national labour law and restrictions on sympathy strikes. Any development of transnational bargaining is also inhibited by differences in the existing structure of union-management relations in various countries. A number of trade unionists in the Netherlands and Belgium did favour a more rapid evolution towards transnational collective bargaining. This attitude seemed to reflect the special sense of vulnerability felt by unions in two smaller countries where multinationals play a large role in the economy.

Many of the national trade union leaders interviewed did note that, as active participants in the work of international trade union secretariats or in some cases European based union secretariats, their unions had supported some proposals for transnational labour relations with multinational companies. This seems to contrast with the lack of widespread interest in transnational collective bargaining expressed in the interviews held during this ILO survey. It reflects the somewhat dualistic role in which the national union leader may find himself. His ordinary role and his union's basic power are established in a national framework. The multinational enterprise can, however, pose some problems for his union whose solution may lie beyond national boundaries. The union leader is more likely to seek transnational solutions when he participates in the work of an international trade union secretariat or similar body.

Practically all of the unions visited have undergone some transnational labour experiences in relation to particular multinational companies. All of them have participated in international trade union secretariat (or related type) meetings bringing together unionists from the same company from different countries. Some partake of a significant number of direct exchanges involving inter-country shop stewards conferences, i.e. stewards from plants of the same company operating in different countries. From time to time unionists may use the data gained from such exchanges directly as bargaining material in their own countries as they deal with multinationals.

While not keenly interested in full-scale transnational bargaining, many trade unionists did favour some process or system which would ensure at least decent minimum labour standards for those working for a multinational company anywhere in the world. This was intended to ensure at least moderate levels of benefits as well as union recognition in countries where unions were weak in relation to multinationals or where government treatment of unions weakened them vis-à-vis multinationals. It was also seen by some as a minimum guarantee against grossly unfair competition in trade, as between the various plants of a multinational across the world.

While unionists felt no pressing need for full-scale transnational collective bargaining devices, in almost all of the countries surveyed dissatisfaction with this or that bargaining (or related) practice some multinational companies was expressed. The issues engendering such dissatisfaction and occasional friction include: problems of obtaining union recognition at some companies; the lack of sufficient protection and facilities for union stewards; companies' preconceived attitudes toward strikes or the nature of the collective agreement; the delays in bargaining which seemed to stem from managers need to consult their home offices; the fear that production might be moved or new investments curtailed, as a company bargaining tactic; the difficulty of coping with specially-tailored wage or job systems, and occasionally special company pension plans.

----

[1] No systematic survey of wages and benefits was undertaken in this study, but see ILO, Wages and Conditions of Work in multinational enterprises (Geneva, 1975).

An overwhelming number of unions favoured some transnational input, or the opportunity to have a greater voice with multinational companies' central management on critical employment and production decisions. They argue that important employment questions are related to major investment decisions which are generally taken at multinationals' central headquarters. A number of the unions had come to the specific conclusion that meetings with multinationals were necessary and that such meetings should be financed by the companies involved.

As previously noted, there was an almost universal feeling that there were great information gaps when unionists tried to understand and deal with multi-national companies. The perception of such information gaps was somewhat less in the Federal Republic of Germany than in other countries, as workers' representatives felt they enjoyed relative advantages via their works' councils and by participation on supervisory boards of many German companies. The lack of a broad enough range of information about the finances and operations of specific multinational companies seems to be felt a bit more keenly vis-à-vis metal working than food manufacturing companies; but in most countries there were no great differences between them in this respect.

Only in a few cases did the unions charge that companies had transferred production from one country to another, to the detriment of employment. There was, however, widespread concern about this practice or problem. Many unionists were familiar with a few important instances where this had occurred, or where a company had made such a threat to help deflect a union demand. The takeover of a national company's production facilities by a multinational enterprise was reported as a source of difficulty or dislocation in labour relations by unions in several countries.

Some obstacles to their ability or willingness to engage in international solidarity action were indicated by a number of unionists. These varied of course from country to country depending on legislation or collective agreement restrictions on the right to strike, the right to refuse overtime work, the right to refuse to work on "struck" production, on behalf of workers in another country.[1] In several countries where such legal limitations exist, the unions are seeking to reduce or eliminate them. In any event, however, most unionists indicated that they were prepared to recommend their members to refuse overtime work where such overtime might hamper the success of a strike against the same company's facilities in another country. They also indicated their intention to avoid accepting "struck" work in their plants.

Most of the unions surveyed had at one time or another been involved in what one might term "home country" sympathetic action. This is that some of them had, on one occasion or another, called upon the union in the home country of a multinational to make oral or written intervention on their behalf, when they had been engaged in a dispute with a multinational subsidiary plant in their own country. Or, on the other hand, many unions reported they had intervened to place such pressure as they could, upon their own management, on behalf of striking or repressed workers (by governments as well as companies in some cases) in dispute with a plant of the same multinational outside their borders.

It was generally agreed that intervention in the home country could be most effective where the home country union was strong and seriously respected by the multinational home office.

Home country type of intervention with management, or similar intervention by a series of unions dealing with the same company in different countries, is often co-ordinated by one of the international trade union secretariats. It seems to be the most widespread and readily available form of intervention by unions seeking to support other unions encountering difficulty with the plant of a multinational in another country. An obstacle to such intervention with the management of a multinational plant is lack of sufficient knowledge about or contact with unions and workers employed at the same company's plants in other countries. The international union trade secretariats and similar union bodies help fill this gap to a degree.

It is difficult to evaluate the effectiveness of this type of "home country" intervention by unions with multinational companies. While the unions, and especially the international trade secretariats have argued their effectiveness in changing management policies in some cases, the same managements often deny that they were influenced by unions.

----

[1] National legal constraints on sympathetic transnational union actions will be dealt with in a forthcoming ILO study of this subject.

Employer experience and views regarding
multinational companies' labour relations

Employer representatives, both of employer organisations and enterprises, felt that the great majority of multinational companies were conforming well to the industrial relations systems of the countries in which they were operating. While there were instances where some multinationals on occasion employed labour relations practices drawn from their home country experience, such a variation might often be an improvement over local practice in some respect. Generally speaking, the more professionalised personnel practices as compared to most national companies were cited as an example of such variations in a number of countries.

Specific labour relations areas in which occasional multinational company innovation was observed by employer spokesmen included the administration of wage systems or company pensions. In several countries some employer spokesmen felt that US-based multinationals often took a firmer line on the observance of "principles" in union-management relations and in the administration of collective agreements, than was the case with the average national employer.

Employer spokesmen felt that proposals for transnational collective bargaining with multinational companies were impractical and unnecessary. They pointed to the way in which this would weaken the authorities of unions and managements directly responsible for plant labour relations by shifting decision-making to remote centres. Moreover, this was contrary to the growing trend in many West European countries whereby the role of shop-level decision-making between union and management was actually increasing.

It was also pointed out, by employer representatives, that there could be a contradiction between union-management bargaining relationships, which were structured along industry-wide lines in some countries in Western Europe, and any attempts to bargain transnationally. As opposed to this is the argument that bargaining on a company basis is on the increase in a number of European countries and this could favour transnational bargaining. The increasing emphasis of unions in some countries on wage equalisation as between occupations and between industries was also cited by some employers as being in potential contradiction to trans-national bargaining.

Employer representatives were generally skeptical as to how deeply rooted were any demands for international bargaining with multinational companies. Experience in their own countries with national union leaders did not lead them to believe that such leaders were prepared to relinquish bargaining sovereignty to international union bodies.

The formidable legal constraints on any possible development of transnational collective bargaining were cited by many employer representatives - differences in laws governing collective bargaining, forms of worker representation at the plant level, employment and social security systems, all of these were cited. German employers were especially insistent on these legal obstacles to any transnational bargaining development.

While employers generally were unfavourable to the development of transnational collective bargaining, some of them were much less adamant in their opposition to the possibilities of some forms of consultation on a transnational basis between multinational companies and unions. Several employer representatives also saw a possible usefulness in such consultation. A number of employer representatives did express concern about the tendency, as they saw it, of unions to publicise massively and exploit such transnational consultation. Fear was also expressed that some unions would try to escalate such consultation to forms of collective bargaining.

*   *   *

There has been some growth in such consultation meetings between multinational companies and unions in recent years. Additionally, a number of companies do report their awareness that a substantial number of unions from their plants in different countries are holding their own inter-country meetings. These meetings are often convened with the assistance of international trade union secretariats for the purposes of exchanging information and possibly to co-ordinate unions strategy vis-à-vis particular multinational companies. These are all indicators of the development of some transnational labour processes.

Appendix I: Questionnaires used during interviews

    The following are the sets of sample questions and issues which were furnished in advance to unions (A) and employers (B), prior to their being interviewed. Both sets were provided to government experts who were interviewed. These sets were not always fully pursued in a particular interview, since in some cases the interviewee was not in a position to answer some of the questions. Generally, the sets offered a useful point of departure.

(A)   Questions and issues for discussion,
    ILO research on industrial relations
    of multinational companies

    1.   Multinationals and the recognition of, or willingness to deal with, unions. Have there been any special problems, as for example in the recognition of foremen or engineers or other white-collar workers? Are there multinational firms which have not recognised unions?

    1a.   Do multinationals afford as good facilities for shop stewards, as for example time off for meetings, facilities for meetings, etc.?

    2.   Multinationals and union experience with layoffs at these companies; cases where there was insufficient notice or information of a plant closing, etc. because of the multinationals "special character".

    3.   Union fears and experience with multinationals as regards production transfers out of the country, and the consequent layoff of employees in the country. Have there been cases where production was transferred out of the country?

    4.   Strikes at multinationals. Any special multinational character? Longer, shorter, over wages or "principles", etc.

    5.   Any special economic or administrative obstacles or difficulties which arise in bargaining or related dealings with multinationals. What labour practices/decisions of the company seem to be taken locally? What decisions seem to be made at distant headquarters, etc.? For example decisions on pensions; must these be referred to the home office of multinationals?

    5a.   What about new agreements or strikes. Do the home offices of multinationals exercise influence in these matters?

    6.   Multinational companies' methods of wage administration (job evaluation, time and motion studies, etc.). Do they import their own methods, etc.?

    7.   Are there differences in labour practices between multinationals which "take over" existing host country plants as against those which have built entirely new plants?

    8.   Are there differences in labour practices between "old" and "new" multinationals? For example, companies that are only recently established in the country as opposed to those established for many decades?

    9.   Are there differences in multinational companies' labour policies that can be attributed to their special technology, for example, automobile companies vs. electrical product companies; hotel companies vs. food companies, etc.?

    10.   Are there differences between multinationals that are due to country of origin; for example, US-based vs. Swedish- or Japanese-based multinational subsidiary plants in the country?

    11.   Wage levels and "fringe benefits" at multinationals, as compared with other firms in the same branches in the host country.

    12.   Union experience in joint or multiple inter-country approaches to multinationals, i.e. with unions in other countries, which bargain with the same multinational companies. Experience through the international trade secretariats, through meetings with shop stewards from other countries, bilateral contacts, etc.

13.   Have there been cases where your home country metal, food or other unions have intervened with multinationals based in your country, to assist a union in conflict with one of this same company's subsidiaries abroad?

14.   Union views and hopes on the possibility and desirability of bargaining and/or consulting with multinational companies on a transnational basis in the future.

15.   Union views on the possibility of international solidarity support in case of strikes which occur at multinational plants in their own or other countries. Refusal to do overtime work? Refusal to handle "struck" work, etc.?

16.   Union views on the usefulness and practicability of applying special international fair labour standards in the case of multinational companies.

17.   Do multinational enterprises change their managers more frequently than do national enterprises? Do the personnel directors of some of the multinational enterprises you deal with participate in regular transnational meetings with similar officials of the same company operating in other countries?

18.   Are there any special information gaps which are encountered in dealing with multinationals?

These are _among_ the questions I hope to discuss.

(b)   Questions_and_issues_for_discussion,
        ILO_research_on_industrial_relations
        of_multinational_companies

1.   Multinational companies' membership and activities in employers' assocations.

2.   Multinational companies and union recognition, including white-collar workers, foremen, etc.

3.   Strike experience of multinational companies.

4.   Multinational companies' policies on layoffs and/or plant closures.

5.   Local versus central (home country office) decision making by multinationals on labour questions, for which issues, employment, investment, etc.

6.   Multinational companies' policies on fringe benefits. Do they "import" such benefits from home country experience?

7.   Wage administration by multinational companies. Whether and/or to what extent they bring in their systems of job evaluation, time and motion study, etc.

8.   Views on the future of multinational company industrial relaticns, including the possibility of future transnational meetings with unions.

9.   The possibility of applying special international fair labour standards in the case of multinational companies.

10.   Are there differences in labour relations policy and conduct as between older multinationals, those that settled in the country before or even shortly after the Second World War, as against more recent multinational settlers?

11.   Are there differences in multinational companies' labour policies that can be attributed to home country origin?

12.   Are there differences between multinationals which can be attibuted to technological factors (auto vs. electrical, etc.)?

13.   Are there any gaps in the information furnished by multinationals?

14.   Do multinational companies rotate their managers more often than national companies?

These are _among_ the questions I hope to discuss.